BITTERNESS ROAD

THE MOJAVE: 1604 TO 1860

"Mohave Indians, valley of the Colorado"
Watercolor by Baldwin Möllhausen. Used by
permission of the Museum für Völkerkunde,
Berlin, Germany

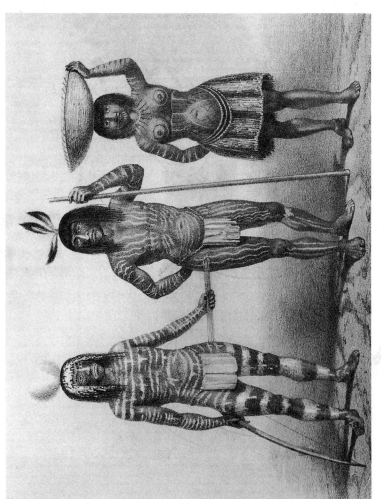

"Mohave Indians"

Watercolor by Baldwin Möllhausen

Ballena Press Anthropological Papers No. 41
Series Editor: Sylvia Brakke Vane

BITTERNESS ROAD

THE MOJAVE: 1604 TO 1860

by

LORRAINE M. SHERER

With Comments by

FRANCES STILLMAN, A Mojave Elder

Completed and edited by

Sylvia Brakke Vane and Lowell John Bean

Ballena Press
823 Valparaiso Avenue
Menlo Park, CA 94025

| General Editors: | Sylvia Brakke Vane |
| | Lowell John Bean |

Volume Directors: Karla Young
                                        Susan Cole

Ballena Press Anthropological Papers Editors:
                                        Thomas C. Blackburn
                                        Sylvia Brakke Vane
                                        Lowell John Bean

Library of Congress Cataloging-in-Publication Data

Sherer, Lorraine M. (Lorraine Miller), b. 1898.
    Bitterness Road: The Mojave:1604-1860 / by Lorraine M. Sherer, with comments by Frances Stillman; completed and edited by Sylvia Brakke Vane and Lowell John Bean.
        p. c. -- (Ballena Press anthropological papers ; no. 41)
    Includes bibliographical references (p.) and index.
    ISBN 0-87919-128-7: $13.95 (alk. paper)
    l. Mojave Desert (Calif.)--History. 2. Mojave Indians--History.
3. Mojave River Valley (Calif.)--History. I. Stillman, Frances,
Mojave elder. II. Vane, Sylvia Brakke. III. Bean, Lowell John.
IV. Title. V. Series.
F868.M65S54 1994
979.4'95-dc20   94-6467

    CIP

Printed in the United States of America.

BALLENA PRESS
Orders: Ballena Press Publishers' Services
P.O. Box 2510
Novato, CA 94948
Fax: (415) 883-4280

TABLE OF CONTENTS

ILLUSTRATIONS

ACKNOWLEDGMENTS

On behalf of Lorraine Sherer, Frances Stillman, Elda Butler and ourselves, we wish to express our gratitude to the many people who have contributed in one way or another to this book. There are, first, the many who wrote reports and journals telling of their encounters with the Mojave, beginning in the early seventeenth century, and the various archivists, librarians, and publishers who have brought the accounts safely through to the present. There are, secondly, the students who assisted Lorraine Sherer—their names unknown to us. We know of them because of the handwritten remarks in Sherer's unfinished notes, for the most part regarding references, "Leave for Dr. Sherer." We thank our own staff, including, over the many years this task has been underway, Barbara Pasch, Katarina Stenstedt, Theresa Cicchinelli, Ernest Quinones, Lauren Teixeira, Pauline Sanchez, Susan Cole, Heather Singleton, and Karla Young. It was they who keyed the typewritten manuscript into the computer, found and verified references, formatted the pages to this size, did much of the proofreading, and some of the editing.

A special thank you is due to Duane Champagne, who guided us through the Sherer collection at the Department of Special Collections at the University Library at the University of California, Los Angeles when we visited it in late 1987. We thank Anne Caiger, Manuscripts Librarian at that department, and the Fort Mojave Indian Reservation for granting permission to publish the manuscript.

We appreciate very much the kindness of Dr. Peter Bolz, of the *Museum für Völkerkunde* in Berlin, for making available the ektachrome of "Mohave Indians" by Baldwin Möllhausen for the cover.

We thank Robert A. Clark of the Arthur H. Clark Company for permission to quote a paragraph from Harrison Dale's book, and to quote extensively from *The Southwest Expedition of Jedediah Smith* in Chapter II; and we acknowledge the graciousness of the publishing firm of John Howell-Books, which has made John Galvin's translation of Fr. Francisco Garcés' *A Record of Travels in Arizona and California, 1775-1776* available to "anyone who wishes" to use it, "with the editor's compliments, for no copyright exists on this work."

Sylvia Brakke Vane and Lowell John Bean

Civic Center Library
3301 Torrance Blvd.
310-618-5959

Customer name: Soh, Wai Peng

Title: Bitterness Road : the Mojave, 1604 to
1860
ID: 32111007252619
Due: 11/4/2011,23:59

Title: The never war
ID: 32111013524621
Due: 11/4/2011,23:59

Total items: 2
10/14/2011 6:06 PM

To renew items go to
http://www.library.torrnet.com

PREFACE

In 1987, Frances Stillman and Elda Butler of the Fort Mojave Indian Reservation, Sylvia Vane, and I examined the collection of papers left by Lorraine M. Sherer that are held in the archives at the University of California, Los Angeles. While doing so, we came across Sherer's unfinished manuscript—a compendium of accounts left by early European and American explorers and expedition leaders who came upon the Mojave villages on the Colorado River. Frances recognized it as a project on which she and other Fort Mojave elders had worked with Lorraine, and as a potentially valuable contribution to Mojave history, but she and Elda thought it would benefit from additional comment from Frances. They requested our help in completing and publishing it, and we undertook to do so, going over each chapter with Frances until she was satisfied with it. We feel the book honors both the Mojave, and their friend of many years, Lorraine Sherer.

It has been a great privilege to work with Frances and Elda on this project, a rare and wonderful experience. We are truly grateful to have been asked to participate.

Lowell John Bean, Ph.D.

FOREWORD

When Frances Stillman and Elda Butler asked Lowell Bean and me to help them complete *Bitterness Road*, we hesitated for a time. We had never attempted to complete another scholar's work and feared difficulties—there was only a barely legible outline for the as yet unwritten first chapter, the references were incomplete, and there were gaps in the data; but we felt reasonably confident that we could identify the various sources that Stillman had not had time to identify, and knew of additional materials that would fit with those Sherer had collected to complete the first chapter, and to fill in other gaps in the story.

Sherer had come to Needles, California as a child, about 1906. Her father found a job as a brakeman on the Santa Fe Railroad, working out of Needles, California, and sent for his family. Lorraine, her mother, and brother, arriving with a dread of the "wild" Indians at Needles, were befriended by a friendly Indian the moment they embarked from the train. As the wife of a workman, Mrs. Sherer found the Indian women more friendly than their non-Indian counterparts. As her friendship with them grew, she started keeping notes on what she learned about their culture. She was still alive when her daughter Lorraine, who had become a professor at the UCLA Department of Education, decided to add to her mother's data and publish some data on Mojave ethnography. Coming to Needles in the late 1950s, she went first to local school teachers, and asked to be referred to the mothers of Mojave-speaking children; the mothers refused to talk to her or to let her into their homes.

Sherer's next strategy was to approach the Tribal Chairperson of the Fort Mojave Indian Reservation, Frances Stillman. Stillman had some reservations about working with this outsider, doubting whether she knew enough, and fearing that Sherer might be a "government lady" who might trap her into saying something for which she might be jailed. Her fears reflected the concern Indians at the time had about government officials, who intruded frequently in Indian affairs. Eventually Sherer won her trust and regard, and they became colleagues.

Sherer's research resulted in the publication of "The Clan Systems of the Fort Mojave Indians: A Contemporary Survey" in the Southern California Quarterly (1965). This was followed by two further articles in the same publication and an addendum to one of them (Sherer 1966, 1967a, 1967b). For all of these works, Sherer's major consultant was Frances Stillman. Sherer and Stillman subsequently began a number of other studies that were unfortunately not completed when Sherer died in the early 1980s. One of these was *Bitterness Road*, which she left without a first chapter, but otherwise fairly complete.

Sherer and Stillmans' manuscript is a compilation of documents written by explorers—the Spanish expeditions, fur traders from the United States, surveyors for roads and railroads, settlers, and U. S. Army officers—who came through Mojave Valley and crossed the Colorado River. Their accounts include both ethnographic and ethnohistoric information, and provide an extremely valuable chronological narrative on the Mojave and their encounters with Europeans and Euro-Americans over two and a half centuries. Sherer not only compiled them, but also annotated them carefully, once again drawing on the additional information provided by Mrs. Stillman and other Mojave consultants, and on a wide array of additional archival and published resources. Remarks in unfinished notes suggest she had recruited students to help with some of the voluminous research required, as university professors often do.

Stillman and Butler periodically met with us to go over each page of the accounts and notes, and to discuss what would be necessary to finish the book. We cite Stillman's comments on these occasions in 1988, 1989, and 1990. We met again in 1993, and consulted often by phone in 1994 to review the manuscript as it approached completion.

An outline left by Sherer suggests that she planned a beginning statement on what the book was about, and another on expeditions before the 1820s. This Foreword is intended to substitute for the first of these. The first chapter of the book, which includes the very earliest accounts of European contact with the Mojaves is derived, insofar as possible, from Sherer's notes. We have added materials drawn from Garcés' acount of his 1775 expedition that Sherer probably planned to use, but that were not in the archival collection. In the chapter on Jedediah Smith's 1826 trip, we have added material from his journal (Brooks

1977), which had apparently not surfaced at the time that Sherer was working on the book.

Chapter VIII was left the most incomplete, perhaps because the story it tells is so complicated; perhaps because Sherer ran out of time. We have somewhat restructured it in order to make it easier for the reader to understand.

Others have told parts of the story of the Mojave and the various peoples who passed through their homeland. For example, Casebier included much of the story in his history of the Mojave Road (1975), but appropriately kept the story of the Mojave secondary to the story of the road; Clifton Kroeber (benefiting from consultations with Sherer) published an account of 19th century warfare as told by a Mojave to A. L. Kroeber in 1903 (Kroeber and Kroeber 1973), but it supplements *Bitterness Road*, rather than covering the same ground.

The underlying story of the Mojave is one that must have been repeated time after time in the course of human history, as advances in technology and other factors enabled human groups to expand, to invade the territory of others, and eventually to incorporate the others into their body politic. Though the defeated people may long retain a sense of their own identity, the history books are composed by the victor. This is unfortunate for our understanding of the Mojave, and equally unfortunate for our understanding of many other peoples in other times and other places.

The Mojave, though a people who welcomed visitors as long as the visitors posed no apparent threat to them and did no damage, successfully defended themselves when the Spaniards, the fur traders, the explorers, and the emigrants destroyed their crops, vandalized their building materials, and in other ways imposed on their hospitality. Their defensive measures repeatedly won them long periods of peace and sovereignty, but they were overwhelmed in the 1850s when the United States Army, its guns, and seagoing ships arrived. Although the military defeat of the Mojave came about as the result of misunderstandings and mistakes on the part of individual Americans, the eventual defeat of the Mojaves as an independent people was no doubt inevitable. They were in the "way" of American expansion—their lands, water ways, and sovereignty a threat to the westward bound. Each resistance was recounted in the media, and their reputations grew at a time when thousands were anxious to travel through their territory to reach the farmlands, gold, and other riches of California.

What stands out in the final tragic episodes that preceded and very shortly followed the establishment of Fort Mojave at the site of the Mojave Villages is the the courage of the young Mojaves who volunteered as hostages in place of their elders, and Chief *Cairook's* sacrifice of his own life in order that the young Mojaves might escape.

Mojave history remains inadequately told despite the efforts of Sherer and others. A window of opportunity exists for scholars to pursue the heroic and poignant story, which tells as much about the oppressors of the Mojave as about the Mojave.

Sylvia Brakke Vane

CHAPTER I:
EARLY EXPLORATION

The first Spanish explorers to reach the Colorado River were led by Hernando de Alarcón, who brought his men up the river in two boats, beginning on August 26, 1540, and spent fifteen and one-half days on the trip upriver and two and one-half days on the trip back to their ships. Alarcón is thought to have turned back at about the Pilot Knob-Yuma area (Forbes 1965:83-89). Late in September that year, another expedition, traveling by land and led by Melchior Díaz, left Sonora to make contact with the Alarcón expedition and then explore the region to the north. Díaz is thought to have reached an area somewhere between present-day Blythe and present-day Parker, but Díaz died in the course of the trip as the result of an accident, and accounts of the trip provide less coherent information than do the diaries of Alarcón (1965:89-95).[1]

Alarcón and Díaz described meeting as many as eleven different groups, but none of them can be definitely identified as Mojave, and it is probable that neither expedition reached Mojave territory. Alarcón was told that there were twenty-three nations living along the Colorado River, each with its own language (1965:97). Although there were varying enmity/amity relationships between the groups, they were not described as being particularly warlike. They were already notable travelers, as

---

[1]Unmarked footnotes were created by Sherer. Footnotes followed by an asterisk, *, have been added by Vane and Bean, as have footnotes cited to Stillman.

peoples were two centuries later, and already had a mixed hunting/gathering and horticultural economy.

Sixty-four years later, in 1604, a Spanish expedition from New Mexico, led by Juan de Oñate, became the first to leave a record of contact with the Mojaves. When the expedition, whose purpose was to "discover the South Sea," reached the Yavapai nation, they were told that two days journey away they would come to a "river of little water" (Bill Williams Fork) that would lead to a large river on whose banks dwelt a "nation called Amacava" (i.e., Mojave) (Bolton 1925:268-271).

Having traveled to the Bill Williams River and followed it to where it flows into the Colorado River at approximately the present-day location of Parker Dam, the expedition came to a halt. Captain Gerónimo Márquez and four soldiers were sent up the river to make contact with the Mojaves (1925:271).

They very shortly returned with two Mojaves, who were asked to bring the rest of their group. They agreed, and said they would also bring food supplies. The next day more than forty Mojaves arrived, bringing corn, beans, and gourds. The leader, a man named *Curraca*, or "Lord," as the Spaniards were told, gave a long speech that was interpreted to be one of welcome and friendship (1925:271-272).

The Spaniards were told that a ten days journey along the river, if they traveled at the same rate as the Mojaves, would bring them to the sea. The Spaniards set out, and for five leagues, along a steep and narrow road where the mountains rose precipitously from the river, saw no Indians. Beyond the narrow pass there was a wide river bottom, thickly populated by Mojaves. Again the Spaniards were provided with food. They were told the sea was nine days journey unless they crossed the river and traveled on the other side, where the journey would take only four days. They were also told that the Gulf of California into which the river opened was not a closed body of water as some Spaniards had thought, but an arm of the sea (1925:272).

The Spaniards judged the Indians along the river as "comely and good-featured" and their women attractive, with skin lighter than that of the Indians in Mexico. The men wore no clothes, but the women covered their loins in skins. When they travelled, the Mojaves carried lighted firebrands in their hands, and were judged to have abundant supplies of food (1925:272-273).

Beyond the land of the Mojave, the expedition, continuing to travel along the eastern side of the river, reached the land of the "Bahacechas," probably Quechans, whom they described as friendly to the Mojaves and speaking a language that was "almost the same" (Bolton 1925:271-273).

The Mojaves, having made an entry into the historical record as a friendly, hospitable people, at peace with their neighbors, were then left to pursue their own ways for another hundred and sixty-five years. But even though people in the outside world recorded nothing of them during this period, the Mojaves and the other peoples of the Colorado River area remained to an extent "connected" to that outside world, because the native groups to the east were involved with it, and both goods and information flowed between those groups and those on the Colorado. Such practices as the growing of wheat were taken up. When the peoples of present-day Arizona and New Mexico had troubles with the Spanish invaders, the Colorado River people knew of the troubles. European diseases spread to them. Since some of the groups in their trading alliances were in contact with the Spanish, the Spanish presence indirectly affected their trade.

Father Francisco Tomás Hermenegildo Garcés led the next recorded expedition to the Mojaves. Garcés was a Franciscan priest, stationed at Mission San Xavier del Bac near present-day Tucson, the northernmost European settlement on the northern frontier of New Spain. He had visited the lower Colorado River in 1771, following it to its mouth. In 1774, he accompanied the expedition led by Captain Juan Bautista de Anza from Mexico to San Gabriel Mission by way of the Colorado River. In 1775, he was ordered to travel with the second Anza expedition, this one headed for the San Francisco Bay area, and accompany it down the Gila River to where it joined the Colorado in the territory of the Quechan nation (Galvin 1967:v-vi).

There had been considerable conflict among the lower Colorado River tribes in this area at the time of Anza's trips, and the Spaniards spent considerable effort on peacemaking between the Quechans and the Jalchedun (Halchidhomas).[2]

A hut was built for Garcés and his party, which included another priest, three interpreters (one of them being Sebastián Taraval), a little Indian boy and another Indian about a league west of Anza's camp. On December 4, 1775, the larger expedition proceeded on its way. The next day Garcés and the three interpreters set off to the west-southwest to spend the next two months among the Cocopas, Halchid-homas, and other peoples of the lower Colorado River (Galvin 1967:14-30).

In February, the Halchidhomas kept urging Garcés to come to their land. He said he would if they would take him to the land of the "Jamajabs," but the Halchidomas, being fearful of the Mojaves, refused, whereupon Garcés decided to go directly to the land of Mojaves, taking

---

[2]Stillman notes that the name Halchidhoma means "driven another way" in Mojave (1993).

a Mojave who was at Yuma with him. He left on February 14, 1776
with Sebastián and the other two interpreters, travelling on the California
side of the river. On February 21, he met

> . . . some eighty Jamajabs who were on their way down to the
> Yumas on account of the news I have recounted. I treated
> them kindly and gave them food because they were very
> hungry. As I spoke to them about the peace between the
> Yumas and the Jalcheduns, they showed me two Jalchedun girls
> whom they had as captives. I asked for them very insistently,
> and finally, after overcoming several difficulties, I succeeded;
> they gave them to me in exchange for a bad horse and some
> other gifts of small value. They continued on their way except
> the captain with a few others, who stayed with me that night,
> sending their animals to San José to drink" (1967:30-31).

Garcés then had to detour around a range of mountains that lay
between him and the river, since the Mojaves told him that his laden
mules "would not go straight up." A second detour was made because
the "Jamajabs were at war with the Jalcheduns" (1967:31).

On February 26, Garcés

> . . . decided to send the Jalchedun girls back to their home with
> my old interpreter, who was to give many messages on my
> behalf and say that as they [the Jalcheduns] were now friends
> of the Jamajabs all the old hostilities were ended. I told my
> interpreter to go on up to the Jamajabs' country and wait for
> me there. The Jamajab captain made a great speech to the
> Jalchedun girls and to the interpreter for the Jalcheduns, and as
> a sign of true peace broke his bow and threw away his arrows.
>
> This day I went eight leagues north-northeast and north
> and crossed a mountain range running northwest. On my way
> down I stopped at some little springs which I named after the
> Holy Angel. Here I met forty of the Chemevet nation. Six of
> them came down, fleet as deer, as soon as we called them. All
> gave me very good mescal. Their dress consists of Apache
> footgear, a garment of deerhide, and a white cap resembling a
> skullcap with a bunch of very quaint feathers which certain
> birds have on their heads as a crest. I judge these Indians to be
> the best runners of any I have seen.
>
> This nation occupies a bit of land, very short of water,
> between the territory of the Beñemés and that of the Jamajabs,
> which then continues along the northern bank of the Colorado

River to the land of the Yuta nation, of whom they gave much information, as also of the Comanches. They are enemies of the latter and of the Hopis, and friends of the Yutas. They said that their nation reaches as far as another river that flows north of the Colorado, and that there they sow crops. They are also on friendly terms with the Tejua Apaches. Their language is different from those of all the river nations. They are close friends of the Jamajabs, and when these cast aside their weapons they do so too. They make baskets very similar to those of the [Santa Barbara] Channel [Indians]. In the various regions where they live, they have different names; they are called Cajuala Sevinta, Cajuala Chemevet, or Chemeguagua. Toward me they behaved very well. They are not given to thieving, nor are they restless. They have much good sense. Besides their weapons they all carry a curved stick [for use in hunting small game] (Galvin 1967:32).

Garcés went on for two days to the northeast and on February 28

. . . reached the territory of the Jamajab nation. To their rancherias, which were on the other side of the river, I gave the name La Pasión. I did not cross the river, but the people came to see me because the captain who was travelling with me went ahead to give them notice of my coming. All who crossed over that day stayed with me, and so to my satisfaction I was able to speak with them on all matters of interest. They gave approval to everything: I should ask permission to stay to baptize them, for they were sure that things would then go well.

I can say in all truth that these Indians are superior in many things to the Yumas and the rest of the Colorado River nations. They are less troublesome, and they are not thievish. They show spirit, and are very obliging; nowhere have I been better taken care of.

I showed them the paintings of the Virgin, which pleased them very much; of the Damned Man they said that he was very bad. I was the first Spaniard to enter their land, at which they rejoiced greatly on account of their desire to know us. They had heard said that we were brave, and they showed extraordinary pleasure at being friends of so valiant a people.[3]

[On February 29] I remained here because there came from time to time so very many. Among them were three captains, one of whom was the foremost of the nation; without him nothing was decided. He came so that I might tell him what was to be done, and he said to me that I would know who he was [referring to his station] when he should have done what I had told him, for his heart was good; he would be baptized and would marry one wife; and he added other good things. This captain is the most important of all and lives in the center of their territory.

These people are very healthy and robust. The women are the most attractive of any along the river. They wear skirts of the same material and design as those of the Yuma Women. The men go stark naked; in so cold a land it excites pity. They say they are very hardy, especially in bearing hunger and thirst, and I found this to be so. It is evident that this nation is on the increase, for it abounds in young people and children while the contrary is to be noticed in the other nations of the river. I was visited by some two thousand persons. Common here are blankets made of woven [strips of] rabbit fur, and of otter which they get from the west and northwest since they are on very friendly terms with the people who live there. They have also been on close terms with the Yumas; their languages are unlike, but from dealing back and forth they understand each other well enough. They speak forcibly and haughtily. I have never heard any Indian speak with more self-confidence than the captain I have mentioned. Their enemies are: on the northeast, the Cuercomache Yavipais; on the east, the Jaguallapais; on the south, the Jalcheduns. When making speeches they give their thighs hard slaps.[4]

I laid before them my desires to visit the Fathers living near the sea; they gave assent and offered to accompany me, for they had heard of them and knew the way. As I was now short of supplies, I decided to leave at once and told them that on my return we should see each other at leisure. I left some of my baggage. The interpreter whom I had sent to the

---

[3]Frances Stillman's grandmother told her that the Indians hid their faces when shown the pictures, and that Garces said, "These people would make good Christians" (1988).

[4]Frances Stillman has never seen this done (1988).

Jalcheduns with the Indians girls that I had ransomed had not returned, so with Sebastián and the Jamajabs for company I left this place.

Mar. 1 54th day

I travelled three leagues northwest accompanied by the principal captain of the Jamajabs, and keeping away from the growing wheat I came to the rancherías to which I gave the name Santa Isabel, where was the captain's dwelling.

Mar. 2

I stopped at the captain's request for the satisfaction of those who wished to see me. This day there visited me another captain with his people, and two Indians of the Chemevet nation.

Mar. 3

I went northwest, with occasional turns west-northwest, three leagues. I took an observation at this place (the rancherías here I called San Pedro de los Jamajabs) and found the latitude to be 35° 01′. Here and at other places further down there are good tablelands for building missions; although they are near the river, they are free from flooding.

Mar. 4 56th day

I set out to the southwest, accompanied by three Jamajab Indians and Sebastián. After two and a half leagues I arrived at some waterholes which I named the Pozos de San Casimiro. There was some pasturage.

Mar. 5 57th day

Setting out northwest, I went eight leagues west by a quarter west-southwest through flat and grass-covered country and halted where there were holes with excellent water, but it was not very plentiful; Sebastián said that watering might be possible in two shifts.

Mar. 6 58th day

I went five leagues west and three west-southwest through flat and grassy country and came to a mountain range [the Providence] with small pines; I called it the Sierra de Santa Coleta. The watering place has little yield and is high up. Pasturage is ample and of good quality. Here I met four

Indians who had come from Santa Clara to traffic in shell beads. They were carrying no food supply nor even bows for hunting. Noticing my astonishment at this, where there is nothing to eat, they said, 'We Jamajabs can withstand hunger and thirst for as long as four days,' giving me to understand that they were hardy men.

Mar. 7 59th day

In the afternoon I crossed the mountain range by a good pass and entered a small valley with sandy knolls at its sides; I called it the Cañada de Santo Tomás. Having travelled four leagues west-northwest (although I would have done better to follow the valley, as it had firmest ground), I halted. At my stopping-place there was herbage but no water.

Mar. 8 60th day

Six leagues to the west-southwest I came to some waterholes with an abundant supply; I named them after San Juan de Dios. Pasturage was sufficient. Here begins the territory of the Beñeme nation (Galvin 1967:33-36).

CHAPTER II: INVASION BY BEAVER TRAPPERS

By 1821, the area of the Southwest had been transferred from Spain to Mexico. The immediate effect upon the Mojaves of this transfer of "ownership" from Spain to Mexico came through the easing of restrictions on trade between the New Republic of Mexico and the United States. When old Santa Fe became a great trading center between Kansas City and Sonora, and between Sonora and California, enterprising men from both countries, with an eye to money and adventure, went into lucrative trading businesses—some to run caravans of mule packs and wagons, and some to furnish the wherewithal for trade (Hafen and Rister 1950:247-249). The caravans that eventually extended trade from Santa Fe across the Rocky Mountains to the Pacific coast by-passed Mojave country above Grand Canyon, but the fur traders and trappers who pushed steadily westward and southward to scour streams for beaver inevitably reached the Colorado and its tributaries. It was then that the Mojaves experienced invasion from the north, via the tributary Green and Virgen rivers, and from the south, upstream from the tributary Salt and Gila rivers.[1]

---

[1]The basic sources for data pertaining to the relationship between the fur traders and the Mojaves consist of journals, letters, and narratives of the trappers who passed through Mojave villages in the decade 1820-1830. Records indicate that the following men entered Mojave territory during this period: Jedediah Smith, in 1826, again in 1827; Harrison G. Rogers, with Smith in 1826 and 1827; Ewing Young, 1827; George C. Yount, in the party of Ewing Young in 1827, alone in 1828; Kit Carson, with Young in 1829 and 1830; Peter Skene Ogden, 1830; William Wolfskill and George C. Yount, 1831. (See Hill 1923; Morgan 1953; Sullivan 1934; Ogden 1933; Dale 1941; Marshall 1916; Cleland 1952; Quaife 1930; Thwaites 1905; Camp 1923.)

Trapping and hunting by foreigners, according to Mexican law, were strictly prohibited (Hill 1923:3). However, stakes were high, and fur-trading companies and organized bands of trappers found ways of circumventing the law. One method was to use the trading license issued by the Mexican government as camouflage for hunting and trapping; another was to risk undercover hunting and trapping without a license. In the Mojave story, it does not really matter whether the trappers who came into Mojave country had Mexican licenses or not, for according to Mojave law no outsider had a right to cross their borders without permission.

The first trapper from the United States to enter Mojave territory was none other than the renowned trail blazer, Jedediah S. Smith, scouting for untrapped beaver streams on behalf of a new fur company, Smith, Jackson, and Sublette (Morgan 1953:189). This new firm was to achieve some note, enough at any rate to obscure the nine-month partnership between Ashley and Smith that preceded it (Morgan 1953).

This was an important mission for Jedediah Smith, because he was now in business for himself, part owner of the fur-trading interests which he and his partners had recently bought from William Ashley, veteran fur trader and their old employer. Smith had grown up in the business under Ashley, starting as a trapper and working his way to the top. In 1823-1824, as commander of a band of Ashley's men, he had traveled from Fort Kiowa on the Missouri River to the foot of the Wind River range in western Wyoming. During the late winter, in anticipation of the spring hunt, the trappers went to the Sweetwater, a Mississippi-system stream, crossed that stream and traveled west to the Sandy, which they discovered by the direction of the flow was a Pacific stream. They had crossed the main continental divide by a pass so gradual and so wide that they did not recognize it for a pass (Morgan 1953). This was the famous South Pass, and this party of Ashley's men commanded by Smith was probably the first to cross it from east to west (Smith n.d., Dale 1941:88). The way was now open to the region of the Great Salt Lake and to the Colorado.

Ashley, in 1824, hard pressed by competition in the fur trade, had substituted a movable trading post or annual summer rendezvous at predetermined locations (Cleland 1952:23-24) for the costly permanent trading post and forts. This innovation reduced overhead, extended

---

[1](...continued)

The original documents are to be found in the files of historical societies, in universities and private libraries, and in government archives. Many of them have been reprinted and made available to all interested researchers.

operations into areas too remote for permanent headquarters, and put a premium on individual enterprise. Small parties of trappers could now trap in the fall, camp in winter, trap again in the spring, and pour into a summer rendezvous to trade their booty. Since each man's pay depended upon the quantity and quality of the skins he procured, this plan gave impetus to production. It also led to dog-eat-dog competition and to increasing trouble with the Indians, as white men edged them out of the trapping business. The rendezvous spread throughout the fur-trade industry; it made possible Smith's access to the hitherto inaccessible Colorado River. Ashley's rendezvous in the summer of 1825 was west of the divide, on the Green River, a tributary of the Colorado. The Colorado River and the Mojaves' valley were now within their line of operations.

In the summer of 1826, when Smith and his partners bought Ashley's interests, their rendezvous was in Cache Valley, near Utah Lake, a freshwater lake south of Great Salt Lake. Rendezvous over, Smith, with seventeen men, set out on August 16, into the unknown country westward, in search of untrapped beaver streams (Smith n.d.; Morgan 1953:194-195).[2]

They had fifty horses, carried seven hundred pounds of dried buffalo meat, other provisions, traps and ammunition for hunting, and "trade goods" to barter with the Indians for pelts and to assure from them a friendly reception (Dale 1941:183).[3]

The two month trip to the Colorado River was one of great hardship. In a surviving account contained in a brief letter to General William Clark, Superintendent of Indian Affairs, Smith wrote that after leaving Utah Lake he "found no more signs of buffalo; there are a few antelope and mountain sheep, and an abundance of black-tailed hares"

---

[2] Sherer's account of this venture was drawn from a manuscript containing copied portions of Smith's journals uncovered with the assistance of Smith's descendants by Maurice Sullivan and printed in his work on Smith, and from other sources as noted. Subsequent to Sherer's work on this book, a copy of Smith's journal that had apparently been sent to Ashley came into the hands of George R. Brooks at the Missouri Historical Society. Brooks edited it and wrote an Introduction for the edition published by The Arthur H. Clark Company in 1977--before Lorraine Sherer's death, but after her work on this manuscript. The narrative from here on has been rewritten to include the additional information found in Brooks' book (1977).*

[3] The original manuscript of this letter, dated July 12, 1827, is contained in the Kansas Historical Society's *Superintendent of Indian Affairs Letter Book.* It has been reprinted in full in both Dale 1941:182-190 and Morgan 1953:334-337.

(Dale 1941:184). Further on, he remarked, "The country is nearly destitute of game of any description, except a few hares."[4]

Smith's party, as it went on, encountered both Utes and Paiutes (Smith called them the "Utas" and "Pa utch"). On the Sevier River the Indians piled up "dry Sedge Bark and Brush" by their homes, and set it afire at the approach of a stranger or other perceived danger. Upon seeing the smoke, the next village likewise set a fire, and so on. Thus the news of strangers spread rapidly. In one apparently uninhabited area, the sight of the "smoke telegraph" indicated to the Smith party that a fairly numerous population had fled rather then meet the intruders (Brooks 1977:50-51, 53).

Smith's route was from the Great Salt Lake to the Sevier River—which he named the Ashley River—then indirectly to the Virgen—which he called the Adams in honor of the President, John Quincy Adams.

Smith's first encounter with probable Mojaves occurred at a Southern Paiute settlement on the Muddy River in what is now Utah (in an area that now lies under the waters of Lake Mead). Here the party was able to buy pumpkins and squashes from the Paiutes. Smith noticed the Indians wore beaverskin moccasins, and had supplies of salt and ochre (Brooks 1977).[5]

> It happened that there were two indians here from another tribe apparently for the purpose of trading for salt and ochre. They told me that a days travel below here this river entered another large River coming from the North East and several days journey Below the mouth of this river they resided where there is plenty of beaver and the indians have horses. I saw on these indians some blue yarn and a small piece or two of Iron from which I judged they had some intercourse with the Spanish provinces. I engaged these indians as guides for I might as well go on as undertake to return. Some of my horses

---

[4] Those interested in following Smith's route to California in detail are referred to Smith, quoted in Sullivan 1934:34. For speculations regarding the possible route consult Hafen and Hafen 1954:112-119, Morgan and Wheat 1954:61-64, Meriam 1923:228-230, or Brooks 1977:35-70.

[5] The quotations from Brooks (1977) that follow are reprinted from pages 64 through 83, as noted, of *The Southwest Expedition of Jedediah Smith*, edited by George R. Brooks, by permission of the publisher, The Arthur H. Clark Company, P.O. Box 14707, Spokane, WA 99214, which retains the copyright.

had given out and were left and others were so poor as not to be able to carry a load (Brooks 1977:64-65).

Smith then followed down the Virgen to the Colorado, which he supposed to be the Green River and which he called the Seedskeeder, the name at that time for the Green. His letter to General Clark continued:

> "I crossed the Seedskeeder, and went down it four days a south east course; I here found the country remarkably barren, rocky, and mountainous; there are a good many rapids in the river, but at this place a valley opens out about five to fifteen miles in width, which on the river banks is timbered and fertile. I here found a nation of Indians who call themselves *Ammuchabas*;[6] they cultivate the soil, and raise corn, beans, pumpkins, watermelons and muskmelons in abundance, and also a little wheat and corn. I was nearly destitute of horses, and had learned what it was to do without food" (Dale 1941:185-186).

When Smith stumbled down from the canyon country into the North Mojave rancherias with his half-starved men and his few exhausted horses, his party had nary a beaver, nor any sign of their trade that could have aroused Mojave suspicions. The country-wise Mojaves took a good look at the bedraggled strangers and, knowing the barren country they had come through, gave them food from their granaries and gardens and permission to camp near their rancherias.[7]

Now let us turn to Smith's journal as edited by Brooks (1977:70-78). It constitutes the first account of the Mojave by an American, not only describing Smith's stay, but also describing Mojave culture in ways that often anticipate A. L. Kroeber and his work on the Mojave many years later:

> . . . In the course of the day some indians met us having some dried pumpkins. finding tolerable grass I re-

---

[6]*Ammuchabas* is another name for the Mojave Indians.

[7]This considerate treatment of strangers accorded with traditional Mojave rules of behavior. "Our people are not the fighting kind. It's the people that live on the plains or the mountains that are hunters. But our people are agricultural, and so we are different. We usually treat people kindly, knowing it's great distances they come from, from whatever direction they come from. So our people always give them food and drink and water and whatever" (Stillman 1990).

mained two days.[8] I killed a Mt sheep and we caught some
pretty good fish with the hook and line. . . .

I had lost a good many horses and some of those
remaining were not able to carry any thing. I got the Indians
to assist me in moving down to where there was several
lodges.[9] These Indians are quite a different nation from the Pa
utch. They call themselves A-muc-ha-ba's and appeared quite
friendly bringing me corn beans dried pumpkins &c which I
paid them for in Beeds Rings vermillion &c. At this place
there is considerable timber on the river and the soil might
admit of making small farms. There was but 3 or 4 horses
among them but I did not succeed in purchasing them, verry
little beaver sign on the river. By enquiry I found that the
principal part of this tribe were 30 or 40 miles down the river.
I remained at this place 2 days during which time a number of
Indians came up from the village below. Among these were
one or two that could talk spanish and as I had a man that was
able to speak the spanish I could hold some conversation with
them. I then moved on down the River accompanied by the
Indians who had come up from the settlements below. The
distance was upwards of thirty miles and the country barren.
On my arrival at the settlement I was treated with great
kindness.[10] Melons and roasted pumpkins were presented in
great abundance--At this time it was low water yet the Colorado
was 200 yards and in the shoalest place I could find 10 feet
deep with a smooth current. The timber in this vicinity
consisting of the Cottonwood and a small species of Honey
Locust[11] with some willow extends entirely along the river
varying in width from 1/2 to 2 1/2 miles in width the river
winding through woodland from one side to the other alter-
nately. Leaving the woodlands which has a tolerable soil the
sandy region commences producing nothing but sedge and
prickly pear. On the East and West at the distance of ten miles
a chain of Rocky hills run parallel with the river and about

---

[8]Apparently in Cottonwood Valley [Brooks 1977:70 n. 81].*

[9]Smith at this point has moved down Cottonwood Valley (Brooks 1977:71 n.83).*

[10]Smith now entered the Mohave valley and encountered the main Mohave settlement. Oct. 15
is suggested as the date of arrival. . . . (Brooks 1977:72 n. 86).*

[11]The screw mesquite (*Prosopis pubescens*), of which more later (Brooks 1977:72 n. 87).*

thirty miles south the Rocky hills close in to the river. This settlement of the Amuchaba's extending about 30 miles along the River appeared quite numerous and paying some considerable attention to agriculture they do not live in villages but are rather scattered over the country generaly whereever [sic] they find the most favorable situations. In person these Indians are tall and well formed complexion not dark. In abilities perhaps second to the Utas. They do not appear much inclined to steal but are quite fond of gambling. Their principal Game is conducted as follows. A piece of ground 30 or 40 feet long and 8 feet wide is made level and smooth. Each man has a pole ten feet long and one of them a hoop 4 inches in diameter. The hoop is set rolling from one end of the floor and at the instant both start and sliding their poles endeavor to intersect the hoop. The one that pierces the hoop or when hoop and poles stop is the nearest to the spot is the winner. The women also gamble by tossing small colored sticks in a dish somewhat like throwing dice. The women are generally very fleshy with tolerable features. The man when dressed at all have a Spanish Blanket thrown over the left shoulder and passing under the right arm it is pined on the breast with a wooden pin. They wear no head dress mocasins or leggings. The dress of the women is a peticoat made of a material like flax just Broken which is Banded with a plat on the upper edge like corn husks. It is fastened around the waist extending down to the knee and constitutes with whole of their clothing. They are in general much more cleanly than the Pautch. They make a kind of earthen ware and in large crocks of this they boil their beans corn pumpkins &c. The men appear to work as much in the fields as the women which is quite an unusual sight among Indians. But few of them have bows and arrows. The bows are 5 feet long and the arrows verry long and made of cane grass with a wooden splice 6 inches long for a head. It is fashion with these indians to fill the hair full of mud and wind it around the head until the top resembles in shap a tin pan. Their summer Lodges about 3 feet high are made of forks and poles covered with grass weeds and dirt flat on the top. The winter Lodges generally small are made in the woods but fronting to the south and where the trees are not sufficiently high to keep out the sun. As the rainy season approaches they throw dirt on the roof to give it a slope to carry off the water and also secure the sides with dirt leaving only a small aperture for a door. As they have not much clothing when the weather requires it they build a great many small fires sleeping in the intervals between them. When they become cold they draw the sand out from under fires and spread it where they sleep. In their Lodges I observed an abundance of Crocks and demijohns. Goards [sic] and small bins made of willow in which they put their corn, beans, wheat, garden seeds, and melons. The Honey Locust in this country bears a pod somewhat longer than a bean. The Indians gather these and pound both the pod and the bean it contains until it forms a coarse flour. they work it into loaves and Let it dry it is then fit for use. When they use it they rinse it with water to which it imparts a sweet and yet tartish taste by no means unpleasant. I frequently observed at a distance from their houses willow bins that would hold 20 to 100 Bushels filled with the Locust pods from which circumstances I judged them not much inclined to steal from each other. Their method of grinding their wheat is somewhat tedious. On a large flat stone a little concave it is pounded or rather rolled with another stone in the shape of a bakers rolling pin until it is sufficiently fine. The stone on which the grinding is done being placed in a sloping possition gradually as the meal becomes fine it is permitted to slide off into a dish at the lower end. The bread which they form of this meal is baked in the sand or ashes under the fire without the covering of Bark or grass used by the Pawnees. When they would roast their Pumpkins or Squashes which is common method of cooking them they take a plug from the side extract the seeds from the hole and replace the Plug by which means they may roast them as neatly as they were entire.

I found in this vicinity no beaver worth trapping for but remained here for the purposes of recruiting my men and horses. From the Indians I ascertained that below the rocky hills that came into the river and nearly down to the mouth of the Gila the country was barren and not inhabited. they also told me that it was about ten days travel to the spanish settlements in California. I swaped my poorest horses with the indians and endeavored to purchase others but without success (One morning an Indian came to me and said the Indians had killed one of my horses which on examination I found to be true. They had killed the horse to eat and took away every thing but the entrails. from this time I had my horses so carefully guarded that they had no chance to continue their depredations.) Believing it impossible to return to the deposit at this season and in my present situation I determined to

prepare myself as well possible and push forward to California
where I supposed I might procure such supplies as woul[d]
enable me to move on north (Brooks 1977:70-77).[12]

Supplied with food and fresh mounts, Smith and his party, after
staying with the Mojaves for 8 days, set out for San Gabriel Mission.
They crossed the river on a raft at a point opposite the place where Fort
Mojave was later built, and traveled west through the Dead Mountains to
a plain and then on fifteen miles to encamp at what was probably Piute
Spring (Brooks 1977:78 n. 98). The next morning, despite finding that
his best horse had been stolen, Smith went on across the Piute Range
where the expedition was forced to camp without water. Spreading out
the next day in a vain attempt to find water, Smith began to think that the
Mojaves had purposely sent him into the desert to perish. Retracing his
steps, Smith encountered an Indian and a boy following his trail. One of
them ran off, but Smith was able to keep the other with him until Piute
Spring was reached again, but by morning this Indian, too, had run off.
The following day the party returned to the river, but the Indians were no
longer there, having left everything they could not carry in their lodges
(1977:78-80).

The party prepared for the worst, "making a pen for my horses
and encamping under a bank of the River which would answer as a
breastwork in an emergency." But in the morning, one of the Indians,
Francisco, who spoke Spanish (probably a runaway from Mission San
Gabriel) swam across. From him they learned that the Indians had run
away because they thought the Americans had returned to kill them for
stealing the horse. To this, Smith replied that he did need his horse
returned, but would not think of punishing all of them for the fault of the
one who stole the horse. All would be well if the chiefs would return the
horse to him. That evening the Indians returned to the lodges. The
chiefs promised to deliver the horse thief as soon as possible, and asked
that Smith and his party recross the river, their being little forage where
they were. They did so, and then moved down the river about ten miles
to the vicinity of present-day Needles, "where the settlement is also
considerable" and most of the Indians lived. Here there were small
gardens where melons and corn were growing (1977:81-83).

The grass at this place was much better than at any place above
and the productions the same as those mentioned before though

---

[12]This passage seems to bolster Smith's later insistence on the fact that it was not his original
intention to go all the way to California, but that it became expedient to do so at this point in his
travels (Brooks 1977:77 n. 96).

perhaps in greater abundance than in the upper part of the settlement. Their wheat is planted in hills. As they have no fences what few horses they have are kept constantly tied by a long halter and at this season are fed on Pumpkins and melons of which they appear verry fond. They ride without saddle or Bridle but by the help of a wide Circingle under which they slip their feet they are enabled to sit firmly. Melons were supplied in such numbers that I had frequently 3 or 400 piled up before my tent. A great many women and children were generally about us. Among the Amuchabas I did not find any verry influential chiefs. He that has the most wives and consequently the most numerous connexion is the greatest man. There was one chief which we called Red Shirt from the circumstance of his wearing a shirt made out of a pice of red cloth which I had given him. He was about 40 years of age and appeared to be a great favorite among the women. He frequently stayed at my tent and slept with any of the women he chose. No Indians I have seen pay so much deference to women as these. Among indians in general they have not the privilege of speaking on a subject of any moment but here they harangue the Multitude the same as the men. While here Francisco came to me and requested I would go and see a man who was verry sick. I told him I was no Physician but these indians thinking a white man could do anything I was obliged to go to satisfy them. When I arrived at the spot 3 or 400 people were assembed but the man was dead. Seeing a large pile of wood I enquired of the interpreter the meaning he informed they were about to burn the corpse which was soon brought and laid on the pile, and also a small bag of net work containing his property. It appeared the man had died from the swelled neck a disorder I think quite common here as I observe many with their necks much scarified a remedy which appeared to have been applied to the case of the deceased as there was a great deal of Blood on his neck. Two or three women were crying and screaming and came to the pile apparently in the greatest agony embracing the corpse. They were pulled off and fire was put to the pile which was soon in flames. The mourners took some strips of Red cloth and whatever they thought most valuable and threw them on the flames. I left them but Francisco told me the deceased had two horses which were already killed and on them the people would now feast. It being a great object with me to procure a guide no means were left untried and finally I succeeded in engaging two

Indians that lived in the vicinity of the Spanish settlements. The stolen horse having been returned I moved to the proper point and crossed over the River for the purpose of making another attempt to cross the plain to California. Having remained at the Amuchabas several days. The first day I traveled the same course as on the preceding attempt and encamped at the same spring (Brooks 1977:83-85).[13]

The Indian guides led [Smith] across the desert by the old trail over which Mojaves had guided Garcés fifty years earlier, and over the mountains which Garcés had named the Puerte de San Carlos, into the San Bernardino Valley, then within the lands of the San Gabriel Mission.[14] Here were green grass and great herds of cattle, sheep, and horses, in charge of Indian herders. The party was met by an Indian steward, taken to his quarters and treated to a hearty meal (Morgan 1953:201). The two padres in charge of the mission visited them and escorted Smith back with them to the mission. The rest of the party followed the next day. When they arrived at the mission, the two Indian guides were promptly thrown in jail,[15] where one subsequently died from the floggings. Of the other, Smith wrote in a later entry of the journal: (December 13, 1827) "I am informed by good authority that my young Indian of whom I spoke the first time I was in California and who was in prison when I went away was tried for his life charged with having piloted me into the country and sentenced to be shot. But Father Sanches, influenced by his own good feelings and his promise to me, wrote to Mexico and procured his pardon" (Smith n.d.).

At San Gabriel, Smith, too, felt the heavy hand of Mexican law, as well as the hospitality of the padres. Called to San Diego to account to the governor for his illegal entry into California, Smith managed to convince him of his good intentions and to escape imprisonment, but he was ordered to leave Mexican territory at once, over the same route by which he entered—which he did not do (Smith n.d.; Morgan 1953:206-

---

[13]Here we return to Sherer's narrative.*

[14]Four days beyond Soda Lake one of Smith's Mojave guides disappeared; but by this time the party had come in contact with the Vanyumes or *Beñemes*, a group thought to have been related to the Serranos of the San Bernardino mountains, and had acquired Vanyume guides (Brooks 1977:91).*

[15]Inasmuch as one of the Mojaves, at least, had disappeared on the journey across the Mohave desert, one or both of those taken into custody were probably Vanyumes.*

Morgan 1953:206-207).[16] In reporting the incident to Mexico, the
governor, Don José Maria Echeandia, attached to his letter the original
of a diary and itinerary which Smith had offered in support of his
representations concerning his presence in California. As a result, the
pages of Smith's journal,[17] which included entries en route from Cache
Valley to Mission San Gabriel, were lost, and with them the first-hand
account of the Mojaves' first visitor from the United States (Dale
1941:191).[18]

In the same fall that Smith entered the Mojaves' valley from the
north, the first trapping party to enter it from the south was setting out
from Santa Fe. On August 29, 1826, the governor of New Mexico,
Antonio Narbona, issued to W. S. Williams and Ceran St. Vrain a license
for thirty-five men to engage in trade in the state of Sonora, which at that
time included a portion of Arizona (Marshall 1916:253). Two days later
Narbona wrote to the governor of Sonora giving further details about this
"trading" party. Approximately a month after the issuance of the trading
license, he wrote to the government in Mexico City, this time informing
his superiors that the intentions of Williams and St. Vrain was not to
trade, but to trap on the Gila, Verde, and Colorado rivers (1916:258).

In all, the party included possibly a hundred men who were
divided into four divisions for purposes of travel. The leaders of these
divisions included Williams and St. Vrain with some twenty men, Miguel
Robidoux and Sylvester Pattie with more than thirty men, John Roles
with eighteen men, and Ewing Young with about the same number
(Marshall 1916:255).[19] These men were all experienced traders and

---

[16] Instead of leaving California via the same route he had used when entering the state, Smith
ignored Echeandia's command. He trapped northward, over the Tehachepi Mountains and up the San
Joaquin Valley. There he left his men and, with two companions, crossed the Sierra and the arid
stretch of Nevada to his camp and Great Salt Lake.

[17] I.e., the original diary, of which a copy was apparently sent to Ashley, and eventually came into
the hands of Brooks.˙

[18] Fragments of the journals of Harrison G. Rogers, Smith's clerk on both expeditions, are
included as part of the William Ashley Papers located in the Missouri Historical Society Library.
No portion of the manuscript covers the sojourn into the Mojave villages in 1826. The first journal
contains entries dated November 27, 1826—January 29, 1827; these cover the period spent at San
Gabriel Mission, and Smith's negotiations with Echeandia. The entries of January 21—28 describe
the beginning of the return journey. (Consult Dale 1941:193-224.)

[19] Marshall obtained the information indirectly from Narbona's letter to the governor of Sonora,
dated August 31, 1826, and quotes the letter as having given the number of this party at about one
hundred men, traveling in four divisions; it read as follows: "Williams and Ceran St. Vrain led one
(continued...)

trappers. William Sherley Williams was the famous mountain man better known as "Old Bill" Williams, who had come to the West originally from North Carolina, and who was the typical mountain man of history and fiction. The others were of different mold, probably best described as business men engaged in the important fur-trading industry. One of these, Ewing Young from Tennessee, had first come to Santa Fe with one of William Becknell's caravans of trade goods. For four or five years, he had trapped and traded for furs in the region of the upper Colorado. The Santa Fe trade caravans had spread reports of beaver in abundance on the Gila and its tributaries, and in 1825, Ewing Young, together with his friend and partner, William Wolfskill, returned to St. Louis for a load of trade goods. Ceran St. Vrain, a well-known trapper throughout the west, led his party on the return to Santa Fe. Miguel Robidoux, one of the prominent Robidoux brothers, came from a proud old St. Louis family. He and his brothers had long been engaged in the fur trade.[20]

Precise documented information with respect to the encounters of these parties is lacking, a situation not uncommon to searchers for data regarding the fur trade. In his narrative written in 1831, however, James Ohio Pattie claimed that he joined the Robidoux party at the Santa Rita Copper Mines in 1825.[21] According to Pattie, the parties of St. Vrain and Robidoux traveled separately, the Robidoux party several days ahead of the other.[22] Trapping was good all along the Gila, near the mouth of the Salt. There the Papagoes allegedly tricked the Robidoux party into an ambush, attacked them, and killed all except Robidoux, Pattie, and one other man (Thwaites 1905:126). As Pattie relates it, the Young party overtook the three survivors on the trail; all except perhaps Robidoux, who was wounded, went back to punish the Papagoes (1905:128-129).

---

[19](...continued)
party of twenty-odd, Robideau and Pratt one of thirty-odd, John Roles a third of eighteen, and Joaquin Joon one of similar size."

[20] Short biographical sketches of Williams, Wolfskill, St. Vrain and Robidoux are found in Chapter 7 of Cleland 1952:246-275.

[21] The degree of accuracy which can be attributed to the Pattie narrative is unclear, for it is difficult to say how much of it is the sole product of Timothy Flint's own fantasy. Pattie's dates in the narrative are sadly awry, and his personal role in the events related has probably been exaggerated. A critical resume of the Pattie report can be found in Quaife 1930:xxi-xxiii.

[22] The Pattie narrative doesn't supply us with many names. Thwaites, and to a greater extent Quaife, the two twentieth-century editors of Pattie, have inferred the names of Pattie's associates on the basis of their own general knowledge of the historical events occurring in the Southwest during this period.

A member of Young's party, George C. Yount, said years later they defeated the Papagoes so thoroughly that they never thereafter showed hostility to Americans (Camp 1923). From then on the three proceeded with Young's party under, as Pattie says, "a genuine American leader, who could be entirely relied upon" (Thwaites 1905:128, Hill 1923:19).

At the mouth of the Gila, the party turned north up the Colorado and came, on the sixth day of March, laden with beaver pelts, to a village of the Mojaves. The inhabitants were terrified at the sight of these men with long guns and steel traps tramping their village, and women and children ran screaming into their huts (1905:133). The trappers marched straight through the village and camped out about three miles above it. Hardly had they camped when a chief with a retinue of warriors arrived to talk with the strangers. The Mojaves, who hunted only for food, and revered the beaver, were scandalized at the trappers' catch of beaver. The chief had no interpreter, but his stern demeanor and his few significant gestures seemed plain enough. He pointed to the beaver, to the river, and to a horse. The trappers understood that he demanded a horse in payment for the beaver. There was no mistaking their refusal when they shook their heads (1905:133).

The chief's next move was equally plain. He raised his bow, let fly an arrow into a tree, and sounded the war cry. Captain Young allegedly raised his rifle and split the arrow, which was still quivering in the tree (1905:133). Reportedly, the chief was now so impressed that he withdrew his men. Each side, however, had now declared war.[23] When the chief returned to the trappers' camp the next morning, the strangers had raised a barricade of logs and skins. Once more the chief asked for a horse. "The captain," wrote Pattie, "bade him be off, in a language and with a tone understood by all people. He started off on full gallup, and as he passed one of our horses that was tied a few yards from the camp, he fired a spear through the animal. He had not the pleasure to exult in his revenge for more than fifty yards before he fell, pierced by four bullets" (1905:133-134).

The next morning Mojave warriors went out in full force to avenge the loss of their chief. They were driven back by the trappers' fire, leaving some of their companions on the battleground. To their

---

[23]"Another thing here was when they didn't do what the Mojaves wanted them to do. They just ran over them. So that's why they didn't trust any more people coming in. The Mojaves also wanted the remains of the beavers to be buried after the pelts were removed, and they wouldn't do it. They just slammed them on the banks of the river, and that was terrible to the Mojaves. They said the beaver belonged here, too. So treat them [properly], you know; take their pelts and bury them. They wouldn't do it" (Stillman 1988).

satisfaction, however, the strangers began making ready to leave. The Mojaves watched them pushing like a war party through the rancherias stretched along the river. Behind a screen of willows and through the maze of rushes, the Mojaves followed them. Above the last village they struck. The outcome of the battle is not clear, for each side claimed the victory. Young James Ohio Pattie, with a flair for the dramatic, described how his group killed more than half of the Indians, and "suspended those that we killed upon the trees, and left their bodies to dangle in terror to the rest, and as proof, how we retaliated aggression" (Thwaites 1905:135).

The other chronicler of the party, George Yount, condemned the Mojaves as treacherous and cruel, but made no mention of a battle or other substantiating details (Camp 1923). His account is briefer and more laconic than Pattie's. This might account for the difference. One may conjecture, however, that if the Mojave found their dead suspended from the trees, it only intensified their bitterness against the white newcomers. They had fought fiercely and later, when some of their chiefs had occasions to go to the mission rancheria over the mountains, they told of thoroughly defeating this party of obnoxious strangers and driving them off in confusion, some in one direction, some in another. By now, the feelings of the Mojaves towards beaver trappers forecast disaster for the next such group to venture into their country. And, before the summer was over, that poor traveler whom they had guided to San Gabriel a year earlier returned with a second party. His fate, therefore, as one looks upon this scene with hindsight, was predictable.

Jedediah Smith, however, was no poor traveler when he returned to Mojave country for the second time.[24] His men and animals were as

---

[24] Smith's second expedition to California is dealt with in the following sources: Cleland 1952:86-69, Dale 1941:183-188, Morgan 1953:334-339, Quaife 1930:150-159, Thwaites 1905:135-144, and Sullivan 1934:26-35, 56, 117-118.

These historians, however, are primarily concerned with themes other than Indians. Their works don't contain a great deal of speculation as to what motivated the Mojave attack on Smith, yet there have been a number of explanations given:

1. The Mexican authorities ordered or paid the Mojaves to let no more foreigners through their territory (Dale 1941:238, Sullivan 1934:173).
2. There may have been some controversy concerning the amount or kind of payment due the Indians from Smith for the help they had offered him on his earlier visit (Sullivan 1934:167, fn. 56).
3. The presence of two Indian women among the whites could have provided the incentive for the Indians to reclaim their women or seek revenge (Sullivan 1934:174, fn. 97).
4. The fight between the Mojaves and Yount's party the previous spring was a logical reason for the Indian hostility towards Smith's group (Hafen and Rister 1950:126, Morgan 1953:239, 422).

fit as the party from the Gila which the Mojaves had recently driven out of their country. This time he would bear watching. Two Mojave guides had gone with him to San Gabriel and one, at least, had not come back. If the other had returned with a tale of the mission guardhouse and his companion's death, or if he had been forced to remain at the mission, the Mojaves could well have suspected the traveler of treachery. In either case, there was little reason for the Indians to accord Smith any special hospitality on his second visit into their territory. Reports and rumors about the doings of white men flew back and forth among the Indian tribes, and therefore the Mojaves must have known that the Mexicans had ordered this man out of the country, that he had taken an offensively long time in departing, and would not be welcomed back. The most serious Mojave indictment against Smith this time, however, was that he had come clearly in the role of a beaver trapper. His dress, his equipment, and the appearance and manners of his men, all proclaimed him to be one. Smith explained the reception he received, so different from his experience on his earlier visit, as follows:

> I went to the place where I intended to cross the Colorado and encamped in a situation where I found good grass, with the intention of giving my horses some rest. I exchanged some horses, bought some Corn and Beans and made a present to the Chiefs. My interpreter, Francisco, from his earlier visit, who was still there, told me that since I left there the last summer, a party of Spaniards and Americans from the Province of Sonora, by way of the Gila, had been there. He showed me some things they had got from them. He said they had quarreled and separated, one party going up the Colorado and the other in another direction (Smith n.d.).

The crossing of the river would expose the party to attack if the Indians should be hostile, but they had given him no reason to suspect hostility unless possibly Francisco, in his guarded telling of the party from the Gila, had tried to warn Smith of the Mojaves' present feeling towards trappers without betraying their sinister plan. Smith, however, caught no under-surface meaning in Francisco's story. His plan for crossing the river was to carry his goods and equipment first to a sandbar in the stream and to make a second trip from the sandbar to the opposite bank. While they were thus making the crossing, some of the men on one side of the sandbar and some on the other, the Mojaves suddenly attacked them, instantly killing ten men and capturing two Indian women in the party (Smith n.d.).

. . . I was yet on the sandbar in sight of my dead companions and not far off were some hundreds of Indians who might in all probability close in upon us and with an arrow or club terminate all my measures for futurity. Such articles as would sink I threw into the river and spread the rest out on the sandbar. I told the men what kind of country we had to pass through and gave them permission to take such things as they choose from the bar.

After making their selection, the rest scattered over the ground, knowing that whilst the Indians were quarreling about the division of the spoils, we would be gaining time for our escape. We then moved on in the almost hopeless endeavor to travel over the desert Plain, where there was not the least probability of finding game for our subsistence. Our provision was all lost in the affray, with the exception of about 15 lbs of dried Meat.

We had gone more than 1/2 mile before the Indians closed around us, apparently watching the proper moment to fall on us. I thought it most prudent to go on to the bank of the river while we had it in our power and if the Indians allowed us time, select the spot on which we might sell our lives at the dearest rate. We were not molested and on arriving on the bank of the river we took our position in a cluster of small Cotton Wood trees, which were generally 2 or 3 inches in diameter and standing very close.

With our knives, we lopped down the small trees in such a manner as to clear a place in which to stand, while the fallen poles formed a slight breast work. We then fastened our Butcher knives with cords to the end of light poles so as to form a tolerable lance, and thus poorly prepared we waited the approach of our merciful enemies.

On one side, the river prevented them from approaching us, but in every other direction the Indians were closing in upon us, and the time seemed fast approaching us in which we were to come to that contest which must, in spite of courage, conduct and all that man could do, terminate in our destruction.

It was a fearful time. Eight men with but 5 guns were awaiting behind a defense made of brush the charge of four or five hundred Indians whose hands were yet stained with the blood of their companions.[25]

Some of the men asked me if I thought we would be able to defend ourselves. I told them I thought we would. That was not my opinion. I directed that no more than three guns should be fired at a time and those only when the Shot would be certain of killing. Gradually the enemy was drawing near, but kept themselves covered from our fire.

Seeing a few Indians who ventured out from their covering within long shot, I directed two good marksmen to fire. They did so, and two Indians fell and another was wounded. Upon this, the Indians ran off like frightened sheep and we were released from the apprehension of immediate death (Smith n.d.).

One August two summers later, eighteen men, half dead with thirst, hunger, and fatigue, staggered into a Mojave rancheria, while their thirst-crazed horses and mules stampeded for the river. It was Ewing Young again, bound for the beaver streams of California. In his party was young Kit Carson, then at the beginning of his career in the West. Whether or not the Mojaves recognized the captain of this band which they had once fought, they knew the rocky, barren country over which he had come. They sold Young a mare in foal, which his men ate greedily, traded him some corn and beans, and watched his party cross the river and disappear into the western desert (Quaife 1935:12-13).

The next summer (1830), a large band came down river from the north. Their captain, Peter Skene Ogden of the Hudson's Bay Company,

---

[25]Stillman notes that the Mojave's ability to assemble a force of four to five hundred men on short notice is not surprising. All the young men underwent training to travel in the desert with very little water. "People [were] just off stream, way up there, to the mouth of Black Canyon and on down. The head man, whom you call 'Chief,' (we call it 'most valuable person'—that's what we call it in our language) had other men to help—three on each side of the river, on down. They were told to be careful and don't start a fight, always show kindness, but when one shows another way, then be prepared. But I think [what gave the Mojave a reputation for being warlike] was—what should I say—the make-up of the Mojave. They're big and tall, like wrestlers. And that's what made them look awful. They look fierce, but they're not. They just look that way because that's the way we live. You know—fiber food! Later they taught us at Fort Mojave to cook with white flour, and it made us stout. And now they say, 'Fiber!' But they (the explorers) called [our food] dirty food and all that. Garcés ate with us, and [his men] said, 'Oh, look at him eating that awful food.' Well, it didn't harm Garcés—it was good food. It made our people big and strong-looking."

She noted that the Mojaves of the last century were big, but not stout. "We have a few now still living that are still just big, but most of them are big and round. It's the 'now' food, you know. We didn't have that—just nature's things besides what we raised ourselves" (1988).

was prepared for trouble (Ogden 1933:9-10). He would not allow the Mojaves into his camp except for two or three at a time. His sentries, guns on shoulders, kept walking back and forth between the Indians and the camp. While it was insolent for foreigners and trespassers to behave in such a manner toward the native inhabitants of the country, the situation was also somewhat humorous. The Mojaves showed their displeasure at such manners by ridicule and mimicry.[26] They swaggered before the camp carrying long sticks over their shoulders, as the sentries carried their guns. The situation might have turned out differently had the trappers appreciated the humor. As it worked out, however, the Mojaves became tired of their fun and took to a more customary way of warning off intruders—a flight of arrows. One sentry was wounded as a result. Instantly the trappers retaliated by firing into the crowd of Indians; the Mojaves retreated leaving their twenty-six beside the river. Possibly the party interpreted this flight of arrows as an attack, which in all probability it was not. History seems to indicate that this was the Mojaves' usual way of serving warning to intruders.

In the early fall of 1830, the Young party returned to California. At least five hundred Mojaves reportedly crowded into their camp beside the river (Quaife 1935:19), possibly expecting good trade. While admitting that the Indians were friendly, Kit Carson, a distinguished member of the Young party, stated that because ". . . they had come in such numbers we mistrusted them, and closely watched their maneuvers" (1935:19). Apparently the Mojaves had left their weapons handy in case their use would be required. As soon as this fact was discovered by the trappers, however, they concluded that it was the Indians' intent to "murder the party" (1935:19). In any event, with most of the party away from camp trapping, Carson took it upon himself to direct the Indians to leave the camp within ten minutes, further threatening to shoot anyone who might linger after the expiration of that time. The Mojaves complied with this order and left promptly, but not without recording indelibly upon their minds one more unhappy experience with white men.

Another brief respite from the trapper nuisance, then another of their old enemies visited the Mojaves, George Yount. He had brought a party of twenty men over the mountains from Taos, crossing the upper Colorado and traveling north of the Grand Canyon (*Wilmington California Journal*, 10/20/1866, as quoted in Hafen and Rister 1950:146). It was midwinter, the mountains were covered with snow, and there was no game. Before they reached the Mojave villages, they had eaten their

---

[26] The Mojaves were excellent mimics, and took pleasure in making fun of the white men in this manner. When offended, they resorted to mockery, taunts, and epithets that generally preceded a warning flight of arrows (Stillman 1989).

last-remaining ox and were consuming their horses and mules. In spite of the big, wicked-looking gun on the back of one of the mules, the "treacherous" Mojave fed them, traded pumpkins for some knives and red cloth, and permitted them to go safely on their way across the desert to San Bernardino (*The Hesperian*, II (1859), as cited in Hafen and Rister 1950:147).

In their treatment of trappers, the Mojaves seem to have considered the behavior of the trappers themselves. In a time when a stranger and enemy were practically synonymous terms, the Mojaves maintained a closed-door policy. Their acquaintance with these trapper forerunners of the United States confirmed the wisdom of this policy. From the Mojave viewpoint, they were protecting their homeland from enemy invasion in traditional tribal fashion. Following the typical Indian concept of no law but moral law, the Mojaves adapted a simple pattern of warning off strangers. First the flight of arrows, warning for an attack itself. Nevertheless, regardless of the fair warning intent on the part of the Mojaves, during this period when Mexico claimed Indian country, trappers and trail blazers from the United States spread the news that the Mojaves were a fierce, cunning, treacherous, and dangerous tribe. No one asked why.

Trapping and trading had been a profitable business, subject to physical hazards for the men and financial vicissitudes for the companies. During the later 1830s, however, the trapping-out of beaver streams and the passing fashion of beaver furs severely reduced the volume of their business. For the Mojaves, therefore, there was to come a twenty-year period of isolation prior to the coming of the first United States government surveys into the Southwest.

Even with the reduction in fur trade traffic, white men were still traveling back and forth across the West. New Mexico traders, carrying calicoes and blankets to California and returning with pack horses and mules, traversed the Southwest. Their route, known as the Spanish Trail, began at Santa Fe, crossed the upper Colorado and the Green, then bent back to follow a generally southwesterly direction.[27] It by-passed the Mojave villages, however, by crossing Santa Clara Creek, a branch of the Virgen, veering off to Meadow Valley wash, thence to the Mojave Desert and San Bernardino.

Some of the former trappers became traders, and subsequently became settlers also. A few acquired extensive land holdings in California, developed ranches and towns, and became "leading citizens." Some left memoirs and other accounts of pioneer days which have

---

[27] Readers who are interested in the specific route of the Old Spanish Trail are encouraged to check Hafen and Rister 1950:155-194.

contributed to our knowledge of California in the years just prior to the American conquest. They can also be credited with fostering the popular notion that during these years the Mojaves ranged and raided the caravan trail across the Mojave Desert and among the settlements and ranchos in the San Bernardino Valley. Fear of the river tribes seems to have hung over the land.

CHAPTER III:
THE SITGREAVES EXPEDITION

In 1851, the United States Government knew little or nothing about the Mojave Indians, and the Mojave Indians, who regarded themselves as a Mojave nation, know even less about the United States Government. The United States had recently acquired the lands of the Southwest from Mexico and had set about exploring their new acquisitions. The Mojave territory was included in this package deal. The Mojaves, however, had no inkling of the paper treaties that had been signed in which their homelands were included. They did not know that Spain had ceded their lands to Mexico, or that Mexico had ceded their lands to the United States.

The first official expedition of the new landlord, the United States, took place in 1851. The expedition was headed by Captain L. Sitgreaves, U. S. Topographical Engineers.[1] He was ordered by the War

---

[1] Lorenzo Sitgreaves (1810-1888) had been an obvious choice as chief of this expedition. Sitgreaves had resigned from the Army in 1836, after having served four years of active duty in the Artillery upon completion of his military schooling at West Point. In civilian life he became a civil engineer, attending this occupation for two years. In 1838, however, Sitgreaves was reappointed to the U. S. Army as a 2nd Lt. in the Corps of Topographical Engineers.

The man who led the Zuni River Survey in 1851-1852 had traveled extensively throughout the Union: he had built roads in Wisconsin, had surveyed the Sault St. Marie, as well as establishing the boundaries between the U. S. and Texas; he had worked in both New Orleans and New York state, had engineered a harbor in New Hampshire, charted reefs in Florida, besides occasionally occupying a position behind a desk at the Topographical Bureau in Washington, D.C.

Lorenzo Sitgreaves attained the rank of Bvt. Captain in 1847, while serving in the war against Mexico. His promotion came as a direct result of gallantry displayed in action against the Mexicans at the memorable Battle of Buena Vista. This is but one of numerous favorable attestations to the man's character.

Throughout his career, he had seen duty in Indian territory: he participated in the "Black

Department to make a reconnaissance of the Zuni River to its junction with the Colorado River, then follow the Colorado River to its junction with the Gulf of California, and to report the courses and navigability of these rivers and the character of the country through which they ran (Sitgreaves 1854:4). To the Americans, the Southwest was a vast, unknown country that separated the gold bonanza in California from the "civilized" land west of the Mississippi.

A clamorous public caused the Congress of the United States in 1849 and 1850 to appropriate money for surveys of the Southwest.

Sitgreaves organized his small party in Santa Fe, New Mexico: one topographical engineer, besides himself, one dual-purpose physician-naturalist, one draftsman, five technically trained men in all, five packers and ten Mexican herders. The Army provided a military escort of thirty men—all that could be spared from their operations against the Navajos (Sitgreaves 1854:4-5).

After a tedious wait at Santa Fe and an irritating delay of over three weeks at the Zuni villages waiting for his military escort, Sitgreaves broke camp on September 24, 1850. His route roughly paralleled the route made visible later by the shining tracks of the Santa Fe Railroad between Albuquerque, New Mexico and Needles, California.

The year 1851 was one of those hard, dry years that occur when nature is niggardly with rain and snow and prodigal with blazing suns. All the way from the Zuni villages to the Mojave villages on the Colorado River, the sun had sucked up the water and parched the vegetation. Drought was everywhere.

By November 5, the men and animals were near exhaustion as the bedraggled party pushed its way over or through or around the formidable mountain spurs about as far west as the present town of Kingman, Arizona. Provisions had dwindled and had to be doled out in scanty rations. There was practically no forage or water for the mules. The physician was incapacitated by a rattlesnake bite, and the guide was wounded in both his head and his hand by Yampai arrows (Sitgreaves 1854:181-184).[2] The Captain's temper was short by the time they found the pass through the Black Mountains that led them to the Colorado River.

Hawk Expedition" in 1832, served almost two years in the Creek Nation during the period 1833-1836; in 1849 he was again sent into Creek Indian territory for a year.

This experience helped prepare Sitgreaves for the intricate task of commanding the first government-sponsored expedition through the virtually unknown, Indian-inhabited territories in the newly accrued regions of the American Southwest (Cullum 1891 I:518-519).

[2] This information is taken from the medical report of S. W. Woodhouse, M.D., who was a member of the expeditionary party. His report is included in the Sitgreaves volume.

The Sitgreaves report gives a first picture of the Mojave–United States relations. It also opened the way for surveys across and through the Mojave homelands—the Whipple survey, the Beale survey, and the Ives survey, all before 1859.

At this point, the river was two hundred and sixty-six feet wide, with six feet of water in the deepest part; the banks bluff and sandy, about twelve feet high, and the current rapid; but a dense growth of willows and weeds prevented me from measuring its velocity with any degree of accuracy. The presence of water seemed to afford the only relief from our former privations, for the soil—an almost impalpable sand—bore nothing but dry weeds and bushes, and the whole scene presented the most perfect picture of desolation I have ever beheld, as if some sirocco had passed over the land, withering and scorching everything to crispness.[3,4]

From this point I had designed to explore the river upward to the great canon,[5] and determine accurately the mouth of the Rio Virgen; one of its largest tributaries; but the exhausted condition of the animals and scanty supply of provisions (the party having been already several days on reduced rations) compelled me reluctantly to forego my purpose.

The whole country traversed from the San Francisco mountains was barren and devoid of interest. It consists of a succession of mountain ranges and desert plains, the latter having an average height of about 5,000 feet above the level of the ocean. The larger growth, almost exclusively of cedar, was confined to the mountains; and the scanty vegetation of the plains, parched by long drought, furnished few specimens for the botanist.

November 7, Camp No. 33. A well-worn trail leads down the river, by the side of which, in several places, were found traces on the ground of Indian hieroglyphics, which Mr. Leroux and a Mexican of the party, who had passed many years among Comanches, interpreted into warnings to us to turn back

---

[3] Sitgreaves is speaking of Union Pass. However, there is another pass to the south of Union Pass called Sitgreaves Pass, despite the fact that Sitgreaves never passed over it. (It was Lt. Joseph Ives who named the southern pass "Sitgreaves Pass.")

[4] The Mojave Indians inhabited this portion of the Colorado River Valley.

[5] The "great canon" referred to here is the Grand Canyon.

and threats against our penetrating further into the country. We had not gone far before Indians were seen in front in considerable numbers who appeared to be assembling to dispute our advance. By the exchange of friendly signs, three of them, mounted on fine horses, were induced to approach, whom a few presents sufficed to convince of our peaceful intentions; and they joined the party and accompanied its march. As we proceeded their number received accessions at every step, until it amounted to some two hundred men, women, and children, who followed on foot, running by the side of the mules, and talking and laughing with every appearance of friendship. In the evening the camp was crowded with them, bringing in for barter small quantities of pumpkins, beans, corn, and in one or two instances, of wheat, which seem to be the staples of their food, for no animals, except a few horses were seen among them; and the few sheep we had left were the objects of great admiration, especially among the women.

The appearance of the Mohaves is striking, from their unusual stature, the men averaging at least six feet in height; and their stalwart and athletic figures offered a convincing proof of the excellence of a vegetable diet. Almost all of the men were naked, with the exception of the breech-cloth. The hair, cut square across the brows in front, hung in loose braids behind, reaching frequently as low as the waist; occasionally it was matted on the top of the head into a compact mass with mud, for the purpose of destroying the vermin that infest them.[6] The only garment worn by the women was a long fringe of strips of willow bark around the waist, and falling as low as the knees. No covering to the feet was worn by either sex. Their arms are the bow and arrow, the spear, and the club. The arrow is formed of two pieces: that to which the barb is attached of hard wood, seven inches long, or one-fourth the entire length; and the other is light reed that grows profusely along the banks of the river, feathered, as usual, at the extremity. The custom still prevails among them of carrying a firebrand in the hand in cold weather, which is mentioned in the account of Coronado's expedition in 1540, and induced

---

[6]"They did that for anything. Just to keep the hair out of their eyes when they're working or whatever. That's when they're working hard and they want their hair out of the way—they plaster it down. For the vermin they also boil mesquite bark that has the sap. You get that and boil it into a real concentrate—thick. And then put it on and it kills everything, [and you] rinse it off. They don't use clay mud" (Stillman 1988).

those discoverers to give to the river the name of Rio del Tizon. Their lodges are rectangular, formed of upright posts imbedded in the ground, and rudely thatched on the top and three sides, a portion of the interior altitude being sometimes obtained by excavation.[7] I saw none of so great a size as those described in the account just referred to.

November 8, Camp No. 34. A large crowd of men, women, and children continued to follow us, many of them carrying beans and pumpkins, and all urgent for us to encamp among them, for the purpose, as they gave us to understand, of trading. I was myself anxious to obtain supplies from them; but their numbers and importunity had been so troublesome the day before, that it was resolved to exclude them from the camp, and to adopt some plan which should free us from a repetition of the annoyance. Before unpacking the mules, therefore, a chain of sentinels was placed around them, with instructions to prevent the entrance of the Indians, and places were designated on the outside where they might hold their market. This arrangement gave great dissatisfaction, and did not fully answer the purpose intended, for many eluded the vigilance of the sentinels, or took advantage of their negligence, and the camp was soon again filled with them. A large number were observed to have arms; and the fact that no chiefs had presented themselves, notwithstanding our frequent demands for them, was regarded as suspicious, and calling for all possible vigilance. The retreat was therefore sounded, and the Indians ejected from the camp, which was accomplished with difficulty, and some old women were vociferous with what we supposed to be their threats and denunciations.[8]

November 9, Camp N. 35 While preparing for our departure before daylight, Dr. Woodhouse, who was warming himself by the fire, received an arrow through the leg, fortunately without doing him much injury. Several others were thrown into the camp and among the mules, but the darkness

---

[7]Stillman commented that one of her grandfather's houses was like that, a house cut into the hill, that looked like a hill mound, but was really a house. "In the summertime it's cool because you're down there. They have a house like that in Bullhead—a restaurant. They copied it from the Mojaves. It's in the ground in the hill, you know. A restaurant" (1988).

[8]To the Mojaves, a hospitable people, this behavior on the part of Sitgreaves' party constituted an insult of no mean proportions.

caused them to fall harmless.[9] The sentinels, however, were thrown further out, and we got underway without further annoyance, a number following us with yells of defiance, but taking care to keep at a respectful distance.

Some days after (on the 16th) we came upon another large settlement of Indians, who represented themselves to be Yumas, and met us with assurance of friendship. One of them, who spoke Spanish tolerably well, informed us that we were eight days' journey from the Gila, and that there was a military post near its mouth, and described accurately the persons of the officers whom we knew to have been stationed there.[10] They were without provisions, living upon the fruit of the mesquit and tornilla trees, and seemed to have recently located themselves upon the spot. I was convinced of the sincerity of their professions, and distributed some presents among their old men; but we did not relax customary vigilance, excluding them from the camp and keeping a few men constantly under arms. The utility of the precaution was soon made apparent, for about the middle of the following day, as the advance of the party was engaged in unpacking the mules to give them their accustomed noon rest, a band of fifty or sixty Indians, approaching under cover of a thicket, fell upon a soldier of the escort who had lagged in the rear, and, having disabled him with an arrow wound in the elbow, dispatched him with their clubs, following it up with a general attack upon the party, in which they displayed much boldness, advancing within easy arrow range, and maintaining their ground against the fire of our rifles and musketoons for some fifteen minutes, when they were beaten off with loss, leaving four dead upon the ground, and carrying off several wounded. They possessed themselves of the musketoon of the soldier they had killed, but showed themselves unskilled in its use, firing it off several times at a distance of half a mile.

Our progress down the river, though heralded by signal fires as we advanced, was continued without further molestation. Numbers of the mules gave out daily for the want of food, until we were driven to the necessity of destroying all the

---

[9]This was the customary Mojave warning of impending hostile action, as described in Chapter II.

[10] This post is Camp Yuma, as it later turns out in the report. The military post was located near the site of the present city of Yuma, Arizona.

spare saddles, blankets, tents, ammunition, books, and whatever was not absolutely essential to our safety. Our provisions, too, became exhausted; and the mules, the poorest of which were daily killed for the purpose, supplied our only food until the 30th of November, when we arrived with a small remnant of them at Camp Yuma, near the mouth of the Gila, where rations were obtained for the subsistence of the party to San Diego, California.

Below the point at which we reached the Colorado, irregular lines of rugged mountains enclose its valley, now receding to a distance of some twenty miles, now advancing toward each other, and at three places abutting against the river, hem it in between rocky promontories, leaving no room for a roadway at their base. The passage of these defiles were the most difficult portions of the journey, requiring long detours over naked cliffs of extreme acclivity, to cross which we were sometimes obliged to break stepping places in the rock for the mules, and to assist them in their ascent by means of ropes, and where a misstep or the jostling of a pack against an impending crag would occasionally precipitate one of them to the bottom of the adjacent precipice. The arable land bordering upon the river is greatly encroached upon by extensive flat spurs, hard, gravelly, and destitute of vegetation, which reach far out into the valley, leaving a comparatively small proportion of the space between the mountains susceptible of cultivation. Some large cotton-wood trees grow directly upon the river banks, but the growth of the rest of the valley is small, consisting chiefly of mesquit, tornilla, willow, and a singular tree with a smooth, pale green bark, and leaves so diminutive as to require a close proximity to discern them. The shrubs are the arrow-wood, wild sage, *hediondilla*, or creosote plant, and grease weed, so called from the brilliancy of its flame while burning. Cacti are not numerous; the most remarkable is the *pitahaya*, or *Cereus giganteus*.

Only two kinds of grass were found, at rare intervals, and in small quantities; a tall, coarse variety, growing in large tufts, and a smaller kind, having a perceptible incrustation of salt upon the leaves.

The trap in some places along the river showed traces of carbonate of copper, and beneath the trap was seen a coarse, gray granite, and in one instance a stratum of clay slate.

Near camp 51, a large rock occupies the middle of the channel, and ledges extend from it across to both banks. In many other places the river is obstructed by shifting sand bars, rendering its navigation difficult, if not impossible, except during a high stage of the water. The water stains upon the rocks marked a height of twelve feet above the actual level, but the indications of overflow were partial, except near the mouth of the Gila, where a large surface appears to be subject to inundation.

Very respectfully, your obedient servant,

L. SITGREAVES
Brevet Captain Topographical Engineers

Colonel J. J. Abert
Corps Topographical Engineers (Sitgreaves 1854:17-22)

Sitgreaves went on to cross the Mojave Desert. By the time the next U.S. expedition came through Mojave country, it was considerably less isolated. The U. S. Army had established a fort on the Colorado River.

The Colorado river was navigable from its mouth to what is now Yuma, Arizona, and could also be crossed there. These two geographical facts had caused trouble for the Mojave's allies, the Quechans, ever since the Spanish days when Juan Bautista de Anza inveigled them into giving safe passage to Spanish caravans *en route* from Sonora to San Diego and thence to other Spanish *presidios* and missions on the Pacific Coast.[11] Here in 1776, the Spanish had established *Mission La Purisma Concepcion*, commanding the river; but, thoroughly disillusioned by broken promises, the Quechans in 1781 had clubbed to death priests and Spanish settlers alike, and then sealed passage to all foreigners (Bancroft 1886:363-4).[12]

After the Indian lands in the southwest were transferred to the United States, and news of gold strikes in California brought fortune hunters hell-bent for the diggings, the Quechans ferried them across the river and traded their crops for white man's imports. The lucrative ferry business, punctuated with minor troubles, brought competition from greedy white men. It begot violence when the notorious scalp hunter, John Glanton, together with his gangsters, muscled into the ferry

---

[11] This statement can be safely inferred from Anza's diary as quoted from Bolton (1930:33-53).

[12] On pages 365-71, Bancroft relates the steps taken by the Spanish to punish the Quechans for this deed. A complete account of this retaliatory campaign may be found in Priestly 1913.

business, murdered an Irish Ferryman, and cut holes in the bottom of the Quechans' boats.[13] The ill-begotten monopoly of these gangsters was short lived. One night, three hundred or more Quechans suddenly eliminated them with war clubs and arrows. The United States War Department took notice, and posted troops at the crossing to protect both whites and Indians. Collisions between troops and Indians followed, and in 1852 the War Department established Fort Yuma, under the command of Captain and Brevet Major Samuel P. Heintzelman, on the site of the old mission. It became a permanent army post which controlled the river crossing, transit up the river, and the Quechans.

There was a time when the strong Quechans and their equally strong allies, the Mojaves, were the big two on the river—the Quechans guarding passage from the south, and the Mojaves guarding passage from the north. Now, with the establishment of Fort Yuma, the Quechans were powerless. The Mojaves knew this. In the story of their neighbors they undoubtedly foresaw what could happen to them.[14]

---

[13] Bancroft 1889:488.

[14] For the most complete details surrounding the establishment of Fort Yuma, see Heintzelman 1852. A short but adequate description of its founding is also to be found in Coues (1900:146-47).

"Camp Scene in the Mojave Valley of the Rio Colorado"
Watercolor by Baldwin Möllhausen
Used by permission of the Museum für Völkerkunde, Berlin, Germany

CHAPTER IV: NEW FRIENDS

In 1853, the United States War Department knew something of the Mojaves and the Colorado River, and knew also that the route Sitgreaves had mapped from the Zuni to the Colorado might be a possible railroad route. The Mojaves knew that a small band of half-starved white soldiers had refused their proffered friendship and the foodstuff they were willing to share in a lean year, and that the starving men had later paid for the rudeness by having to eat their bony mules before they reached Fort Yuma.

The Mojaves' second experience with a United States expedition, in 1853-54, removed the bitter taste. The largest scientific expedition was commanded by Lieutenant A. W. Whipple, Topographical Engineers, United States Army. His order from the War Department was to find a practical route for a railroad along the 35th parallel from the Mississippi River to the Pacific Ocean.[1] Whipple was assisted by Brevet Second Lieutenant J. C. Ives, a topographical engineer, and Second Lieutenant D. S. Stanley, who acted as quartermaster and commissary.

---

[1] See the official orders of Jefferson Davis, Secretary of War, to Lt. Amiel Weeks Whipple, dated May 14, 1853, as they appear in Whipple 1856:Part I, "Itinerary," pp. 1-2.

There are four parts of the Whipple report: besides the "Itinerary" section, there are three other parts, respectively concerning geological observations taken on the expedition, topographical information, and anthropological data obtained on the various Indian tribes encountered. For our purposes, however, we are primarily concerned only with the "Itinerary" section of the document.

Whipple was a seasoned surveyor and a student of Indian life.[2] His mission required a comprehensive survey of the lay of the land, a study of its lumber and mineral resources, its vegetation and water supply, and of the Indian tribes through whose lands the proposed railroad would cross. He had had the recent unpleasant experience of working under J. R. Bartlett on the long, drawn-out, and controversial Mexican Boundary Survey and knew what lack of adequate surveying equipment, lack of understanding of the Indian customs, and a profusion of political appointees could do.[3] He managed to secure an appointment by the Secretary of War, Jefferson Davis, that would give him not only competent scientific help for each of the tasks assigned to his mission, but a team who could work and live together compatibly under grueling circumstances.   He was equally selective in picking good cooks, muleteers, and packers who knew their job and could keep out of trouble.[4] His policy, clearly understood and followed to the letter by his

---

[2] Amiel Weeks Whipple (1816-1863), a native of Massachusetts, attended Amherst College and the U.S. Military Academy at West Point, graduating as a 2nd Lt. in 1841. He transferred from the Artillery to the Corps of Topographical Engineers in this same year. In the early stages of his career, Whipple served as a hydrographic engineer in Maryland, New Orleans, La., and Portsmouth, N. H. He was engaged in surveying the northeastern boundary of the United States with the British Provinces, was a member of the Weller Boundary Commission, and in 1850 joined the Mexican Boundary Commission under Bartlett as chief astronomer, as well as taking care of the surveying duties. He completed his duty with Bartlett in 1852.

After Whipple's expedition for a railroad route from the Mississippi River to the Pacific Ocean during the year 1853-1856, he served as a light-house superintendent in the Great Lake region. He helped open the lakes to navigation.

Whipple became a hero in the Civil War. He was decorated for bravery in action against the enemy on at least three different occasions: at the Battle of Manassas, the Battle of Fredericksburg and the Battle of Chancellorsville, where he was fatally wounded on the second day of fighting. He died in Washington, D.C. a short time later, but not before being promoted to the rank of Major General for his gallantry.

Two military establishments were named in his honor: Whipple Barracks, Prescott, Arizona (1869-1884); and Fort Whipple, now part of the Fort Myer Reservation near Washington, D.C. (1863) (Cullum 1891 II:65-66; Foreman 1941:7-9).

[3] The Mexican Boundary Survey (see Goetzman 1959, Chapter 5) was a result of the Treaty of Guadalupe Hidalgo, signed on February 2, 1848. This treaty put an end to the war between the United States and Mexico.

[4] Those who were assigned to the Whipple expedition by the U. S. War Department included: J. M. Bigelow, M.D. of Ohio, surgeon and botanist; Jules Marcou of Massachusetts, geologist and mining engineer; C. B. R. Kennerly, M.D. of Virginia, physician and naturalist; A. H. Campbell of Virginia, principal assistant railroad engineer; H. B. Möllhausen of the District of Columbia, topographer and artist; Hugh Campbell of Texas, assistant astronomer; William White, Jr. of Pennsylvania, assistant meteorological observer and surveyor; George Gibson Garner of Maryland,

(continued...)

men, was to treat Indians as human beings, to respect their customs and their property, to commit no wrongs and to submit to none (Whipple 1856:120).

He saw to it that his outfit was equipped with the best of surveying instruments, durable wagons and camping equipment, good mules and horses, ample commissary supplies, and a plentiful stock of merchandise selected to appeal to Indians.

The expedition left Fort Smith on the Mississippi River with a train of twelve wagons, each drawn by six mules. In addition to two hundred mules, the caravan included a herd of beef cattle and a flock of sheep. It was accompanied by a disciplined military escort of seventy men (1856:5).

Whipple's itinerary from Fort Smith to Albuquerque, New Mexico, is not relevant to the Mojave story. We begin at Albuquerque, where the expedition bivouacked for more than a month (October 6 to November 10). General Garland, commanding the department, was absent on a tour of inspection, and the acting commissary officer was unwilling to issue supplies without the approval of his superior officer (1856:48). Here the men worked by day, and by night reveled in the hospitality of Señors, Señoras, and Señoritas.

At the same time, while waiting, they gathered all the information they could about the country ahead of them. They had, of course, Sitgreaves' map and notes, a copy of Walker's route in 1851, and first-hand information from one of Aubrey's men about his travels.[5] Here

---

[4](...continued)
assistant astronomer and secretary; N. H. Hutton of the District of Columbia, assistant engineer; John P. Sherburne of New Hampshire, assistant meteorological observer and surveyor, Thomas H. Parke of Pennsylvania, assistant astronomer and computer; and Walter Jones, Jr. of the District of Columbia, assistant surveyor.

[5] Joseph Walker and Francis X. Aubrey were "mountain men": adventurers, seekers after fortune. Walker explored the regions of the Southwest as early as 1833 under order of Capt. B. L. E. Bonneville (who later reaped the credit for Walker's discoveries). Walker was a trapper, and his expedition's prime interest had been furs. However, Walker's party was the first to traverse the route that became the first emigrant road to California (Goetzman 1959:52). In the years 1843-1844, Walker had accompanied Fremont's expedition into this country. Fremont spoke of him thus: "Mr. Joseph Walker, our guide . . . has more knowledge of these parts than any man I know" (Goetzman 1959:100; Goetzman quotes Fremont's own report of this expedition on p. 395). Whipple crossed through the same general territory that Walker had traveled only two years previously, in 1851, although the routes of the two men were not exactly the same.

Aubrey, on the other hand, was a private trader who was widely known under the label, "skimmer of the plains." He had traveled over the so-called "middle route" (because it ran between the Old Spanish Trail to the north, and the Old Gila Trail to the south) from New Mexico to California in 1852, a year before Whipple. As Whipple was traipsing westward in 1853, Aubrey was
(continued...)

Whipple engaged two veteran guides, Antoine Leroux, who had guided Sitgreaves, and Jose Manuel Savedra, a New Mexican, who had once accompanied a Moqui war party against the Mojaves. He also added reinforcements from Fort Defiance to his escort (Whipple 1856:48).

During the winter months of 1853, the survey labored through rain, snow, and ice over the route mapped by Sitgreaves.

The party usually worked in two divisions. Lieutenant Ives was responsible for the astronomical and meteorological observations, determination, and records. He was also in charge of the wagon train that carried provisions, instruments, technological supplies, tents, tools, weapons, and ammunitions. In his train, most of the time, were the assistant astronomers and the assistant meteorological observers and surveyors.

Whenever the first division of the train camped, Lieutenant Whipple and the scientists, or some of them, made reconnoitering trips in the vicinity, observing grades, timber, stone, and other resources for railroad building. Doctors Bigelow and Kennerly collected flora and fauna, Mr. Marcou studied strata and collected mineral specimens, and Mr. Möllhausen sketched. When they reached a decision as to the suitability of the route in each vicinity, they signaled or sent back for the train to come up and camp, and on the way Lieutenant Ives took his observations and made the surveys.

The route surveyed by Whipple was approximately that of the Santa Fe railway today, running west through such modern towns as Winslow, Flagstaff, and Ashfork. About halfway between today's Ashfork and Seligman, Whipple left Sitgreaves' route and turned due south to Pecacho Spring (Pecacho Buttes on today's map), hoping to find a better route. The remainder of his itinerary was southwest until the men reached the river called Bill Williams Fork—the river Sitgreaves described as flowing into the Colorado River. This led them to their first view of the Colorado in the neighborhood of today's Parker Dam.

After a brief period in "the beautiful valley of the Chemehuevis" (Whipple 1856:112)—which now lies deep under the waters of Lake Havasu since the building of Parker Dam—Whipple and his expedition advanced to the border of Mojave territory.

---

[5](...continued)
setting out in an easterly direction from Tejon Pass, California, on a volunteer survey of northern Arizona to establish a railroad route; today's Santa Fe follows the same line indicated by Aubrey. However, even though Aubrey had blazed a trail through the same country as Whipple, his was also not the exact route taken by Whipple in 1853-1854 (Beale 1858:2).

The Mojaves knew that this big, friendly trading expedition was headed toward their southern border, just as they had known in 1851 that a small scouting party of foreigners (the Sitgreaves reconnoiter) was advancing toward their northern border.   Mojave scouts entered Whipple's camp long before the expedition reached their homeland.[6] What they saw and heard was *ahota*, good, and this news they relayed to their people.

The years 1852-53, unlike the drought years of 1851 when Sitgreaves entered the Mojave Valley, were bountiful years. Fed by the melting snows that had lain full on the mountains, the Colorado overflowed its banks. The Mojaves' stomachs were filled, their granaries held surplus to spare, and their spring gardens were planted. The signs were auspicious as Whipple and his expedition prepared to leave the "Valley of the Chemehuevis"[7] and trust themselves to the Mojaves.

The artist-topographer of the expedition, Baldwin Möllhausen, wrote of Mojaves visiting the expedition in Chemehuevi Valley on February 22:

> On the 22nd of February we continued our journey northward, at some distance from the Colorado, and towards noon reached the river, along whose banks we travelled till towering masses of rock stretching far into the country seemed to bar our way. We pitched our camp, therefore, in order to debate on the course we were to take, for we had not yet reached the actual village of the Mohave Indians, although numerous parties from it had visited us. As far as we had hitherto seen of the Colorado, dry stony ground and bare rocks

---

[6] An advanced contingency of Mojaves met the Whipple group on February 21, two days prior to the party's entry into Mojave country (Whipple 1856:110).

[7] "[This valley] was Chemehuevi Valley; now it's just Chemehuevi Landing—just a little strip left, but they're living there. It was a nice valley, but to us it's our sacred place, where the departed spirits meet, coming down from up above. That's why we didn't live there. We could live on the east side. That's where Whipple found our people, near Bill Williams Valley, when he was coming down. When Sitgreaves was coming, trying to find a way to the Pacific Ocean to lay the railroad, he got lost, and came down the big sand and landed down in the valley there at the Bill Williams River. He found Mojaves there, but they were on the east side, not the west. It was the Paiutes that came across the river at that time, and that's where Whipple saw them. The Mojaves called them Chemehuevis—that's the name we gave them. It means "work with the fish, to get the fish, to eat fish." That's what the word is—Chemehuevi.

"We were not going to live there, [and] we wanted to get them off the desert, and to live there in that valley. Besides, there's other game there, like rabbits and things. So that's why [we let them live in that valley]" (Stillman 1988).

alternated with valleys, fertile, though of small extent. In these valleys or lowlands, the Indians live hidden in mezquit woods and appear to obtain from the fruitful soil all that they desire or need, for besides those fruits of the earth, for which they have partly to thank their own industry, they have the mezquit tree itself, which, in years of bad harvest, affords them valuable help.

Many Indians visited us this day in our new camp, watched curiously all our doings, and laughed and shouted at all that appeared extraordinary. Now that they were at peace they were the most innocent, well-meaning fellows in the world. While we were talking, as well as we could, with some of the men, we became aware of the approach of a whole troop of others with their women and children, who were advancing from the rocky chain towards us in solemn procession. They were Mohave Indians, who came in a spirit of commercial enterprise to enter on a barter trade with various articles; and though they were little, or not at all dressed, the troop had a very gay appearance, as, led by a chief, it entered our encampment. The herculean forms of the men, with their hair dressed with white, blue, red, and yellow paint, and hanging down to their feet, their brilliant eyes flashing like diamonds—looked even taller than they were from the plumes of swans', vultures', or woodpeckers' feathers that adorned their heads. Some wore as their sole garment a fur mantle, made of hares' or rats' skins, thrown over their shoulders; but one outshone all the rest of the company, having picked up an old waistcoat that had been thrown or bartered away by some of our people, and now displayed it for the completion of a costume that had hitherto consisted only of paint. The women all wore the peculiar petticoat above mentioned, the front of which the ladies of most distinction had made of twisted woollen cords, instead of strips of bast. They carried on their heads clay vessels, bags made of bast, and water-tight baskets filled with the productions of their fields and of their own industry. When they reached the camp, the women knelt down in rows on the ground, and placed their full baskets before them, while the men who had accompanied them scattered themselves about the camp, challenged our people to trade, and sometimes watched the fulfillment of a bargain. This went on till late in the evening, when most of the Indians were, for the sake of security, required to quit the camp and the watch fires; but many of the number had retired to their huts and caves as soon as it began to grow cool (Möllhausen 1858:249-251).

Let Whipple pick up the narrative:[8]

From the Chemehuevis to the Mojave Valley, on the Colorado
February 23, Camp 130. The beautiful valley of the Chemehuèvis Indians is about five miles broad, and eight or ten miles in length. As we ascended the eastern edge, we saw numerous villages and a belt of cultivated fields upon the opposite bank. Great numbers of the natives swam the river and brought loads of grain and vegetables. The chief begged us to encamp again within the limits of his territory, to enable his people to trade; but, as we could not, the poor Indians were obliged to turn homewards with their heavy burdens. The chief alone accompanied us; and, after travelling between eleven and twelve miles, we encamped upon the coarse but abundant grass of the valley.

Waiting at this place was a Mojave chief, with his band of warriors, to welcome us to their country. With eyes cast to the ground, and in silence, he submitted to the ceremony of an introduction. With apparent indifference he received the few presents that were offered, and then quietly watched the trading of his people. It was now evident why the Chemehuèvis would not follow us with their articles of traffic to camp. They feared to encroach upon the privileges of the Mojaves. The trade commenced by the offer of a basket of maize for three strings of white porcelain beads. No sooner was the bargain concluded, than the whole multitude crowded in to dispose of their produce at the same price. Delighted at their bargains, they were exceedingly merry. But the acting quartermaster, not wishing to dispose of all of the beads, hid a part, and tried to induce them to trade for other things. They understood the operation, refused all offers, and were silent for half an hour. Then they rose *en masse*, took up their grain, and were about to leave; when, after an explanation, the spirit of trade was restored, and calico being established as currency, became as popular as beads had been. We purchased in a short time about

---

[8] Grant Foreman has edited the complete itinerary reports of Whipple for the years 1853-1854, in Foreman 1941. The introduction to his book is especially useful in clarifying and explaining the many aspects of the Whipple expedition.

six bushels of maize, three bushels of beans, and considerable wheat, besides squashes and peas. At sunset the Indians seemed happy as possible, and made arrangements for passing the night with us. But their acquaintance was deemed of too short duration to entitle them to such confidence, and all, except the chief and a few of his friends, were driven reluctantly from camp. Some of them were considerably exasperated, but they went quietly enough and built their fires just beyond the line of sentinels. Those remaining did not once lie down during the whole night, but sat at the fire using wood at the cook's expense. Indians always expect to be waited upon by the servants of white people.

During the evening there came into camp a young fellow, asking for the captain. At the first glance he was recognized as an old acquaintance, from the Algodones below the mouth of the Rio Gila, where I had seen him a year since. He is a Cuchan;[9] and, at that time, his people were at war with our troops, and kept aloof upon the opposite side of the river. But José, (that is the name he assumed,) putting confidence in us, swam the river, and led our train to the place where there were boats for crossing the Colorado. We found him a shrewd lad, and he proved considerable service to the party.

The sky has been partially overcast, but the usual set of astronomical and magnetic observations were taken. Near the termination of the day's march, the trail passed among hills where a little work would make a wagon road. A better route would doubtless follow the bank of the Colorado. These hills are scarcely worth mentioning in connection with the prospects for a railway, as it would be easy to pass along the base of the bluffs that border the river.

February 24, Camp 131. The Indians seemed to have recovered from the annoyance of being turned from camp last night, and again became lively and good-humored, cheerfully answering our questions regarding the way before us. A short distance from camp was seen a second mountain spur, intersecting the valley, similar to the one where we had deserted the wagons. The chief told us that the trail traversing it was rough, and impassable for the spring-carriage. After much consideration, the natives informed us that, by turning to the right, the

---

[9] The words "Cuchan", "Quechan," and "Yuma" are merely different denotations for the same tribe of Indians.

ridge could be entirely avoided; and two of them consented to act as guides, to conduct the surveying party by that route. With the pack-mules we kept the old trail, that led through ravines, and over hills, to avoid the bluffs upon the river-bank. The path in some places passed through deep chasms, and over precipices of porphyritic rocks. The mules tumbled headlong, became weary and dizzy, and four were left upon the roadside. Having travelled about ten miles, we emerged from the hills, descended by an arroyo to the river, and were gladdened by a sight of the great valley of the Mojaves. Ascending it a short distance, we joined the surveying party, and encamped; Lieutenant Tidball, with a portion of the escort, being still in advance. Again we have experienced the advantage of having cultivated a kindly feeling with the natives. Our parties to-day have necessarily been scattered widely, and an attack by Indians would have proved disastrous to the expedition. But instead of impeding our operations, they have rendered good service, giving valuable information and faithful guidance. The trail of the surveying party conformed strictly to the account given by the guides—passing over a smooth prairie country, without encountering a hill. But to avoid the circuit which it made, a road might be constructed along the bank, to a narrow gorge, where the spurs upon either side came down to the water's edge. There the position is favorable for bridging the river, and from thence the valley would be ascended upon the west side.

We have had, to-day, violent wind from the north. It filled our eyes with sand, and added much to the labor of driving the mules, and replacing the oft-broken packs.

February 25, Camp 132. We continued the survey about a mile along the border of the fine valley, to Lieutenant Tidball's camp. Here, finding a large field which had been burned, and fresh grass springing from the roots, we turned our mules loose, to graze and rest from the fatigue of yesterday's march. Indians collected, and we were informed that one of the great captains was coming to visit us. A few hundred yards distant was seen an assemblage, and soon a long procession of warriors approached, headed by the chief and his interpreter, our Cuchan friend José. The latter with great formality introduced the distinguished dignitary of the Mojave nation, who returned our salutations with gravity becoming his rank.

He then presented his credentials from Major Heintzelman;[10] who stated that the bearer, Captain Francisco, had visited Fort Yuma with a party of warriors, when upon an expedition against the Cocopas, and professed friendship; but he advised Americans not to trust him. The parade and ceremony were not, upon this occasion, as vain and useless as might be supposed, for without them we should have taken this great chief for the veriest beggar of the tribe. He was old, shrivelled, ugly, and naked, except a strip of dirty cloth suspended by a cord around his loins, and an old black hat, bandless and torn, drawn down to his eyes. Judging from his half stupid, half ferocious look, one might suspect that there had been foul play towards the former owner of the hat. But his credentials being satisfactory, he was received, and seated on a blanket at our right. The pipe was passed around; the object of our visit explained, and a guide asked, to conduct us to the intersection of the Mormon road with the Mojave river.[11] He replied that it was all well; none of his people would commit depredations upon our property, but would afford all the aid in their power. A few trinkets, some tobacco, and red blankets cut into narrow strips for head-dresses, were then presented for distribution among the warriors. As the chief would accept nothing for himself, the council was dissolved. Then commenced the trade for grain, and the scene suddenly changed from grave decorum to boisterous merriment and confusion. Savedra counted six hundred Indians in camp, and probably half of them had brought bags of corn or baskets of meal for sale. The market was established; and all were crowding, eager to be the first at the stand, amid shouts, laughter, and a confusion of tongues—English, Spanish, and Indian. The result was, the acquisition by us of about six bushels of corn and two hundred pounds of flour, and the supply was not exhausted. There must have been at least ten bushels of beans for sale, and great numbers of pumpkins, some two feet in diameter, and weighing

---

[10] The paper of introduction was very important to the Mojaves, who were forced to rely on their contents without being able to read the credentials themselves. Four such testimonial letters, written between 1861–1888 by commanders at Fort Mojave, near Needles, California, are carefully preserved in the tribal records of the Mojaves.

[11] The Indian guide directed them skillfully to a point near Barstow, California (Camp 1923:146), to the intersection with the Mormon Road, which was also known as the Old Spanish Trail. Here, the guide took leave of the Whipple group, which then proceeded onward to Cajon Pass.

perhaps twenty-five pounds.[12] They receive, in exchange, in
order of preference, small white or large blue beads; red
blankets cut into strips six inches wide; white cotton cloth; and
calico, in pieces three or four yards in length. Other articles
and trinkets they esteem of no value. When the trading was
concluded, they ranged about camp in picturesque and merry
groups, making the air ring with peals of laughter. Some of the
young men selected a level spot, forty paces in length, for a
play-ground, and amused themselves in their favorite sport with
hoop and poles. The hoop is six inches in diameter, made of
an elastic cord. The poles are straight, and about fifteen feet in
length. Rolling the hoop from one end of the course, two
persons chase it half way, and at the same instant throw their
poles. He who succeeds in piercing the hoop wins the game.

Target firing and archery were then practiced—our own
people firing with rifles and Colt's pistols, and the Indians
shooting arrows. Fortunately, the fire-arms were triumphant;
and finally an old Mojave, in despair at their want of success,
ran in hot haste and tore down the target. It is said that several
sad-looking fellows in the crowd are slaves, prisoners taken in
the last expedition against the Cocopas. In the military code of
this people, a captive is forever disgraced. Should he return to
his tribe, his own mother would discard him as unworthy of
notice. There are only two Cuchans here, Jose and his friend;
others are said to be on their way hither. The chief, Manuel,
informs us that the object of their visit is to obtain a fresh
supply of provisions, their own grain and vegetables having
been exhausted in trade with the troops at Fort Yuma.

Notwithstanding the unity of language, the family
resemblance, and amity which exists between Cuchans and
Mojaves, there is exhibited on the part of the latter a jealousy
similar to that witnessed among Pimas and Maricopas towards
each other. An instance of this feeling occurred this evening.
A woman caught her little son endeavoring to conceal some
trinket that he fancied. She snatched the article from him with
a blow and a taunt, saying, "Oh, you Cuchan!" Some one

---

[12]That the Mojaves had pumpkins in February shows the efficiency of their storage system.
"They wrapped pumpkins and melons to keep them from touching each other, and buried them in
the ground. When they needed them, they knew just where they were and got them one at a time.
They cut meat, and sometimes pumpkins, in strips and dried the strips in the sun. Later they soaked
them before they cooked them. They were good" (Stillman 1989).

inquired if he belonged to that tribe. "Oh, no," she replied, "he
is a Mojave, but behaves like a Cuchan, whose trade is stealing."

These Indians are probably in as wild a state of nature
as any tribe now within the limits of our possessions. They
have not had sufficient intercourse with any civilized people to
acquire a knowledge of their language or their vices. Leroux
says that no white party has ever before passed them without
encountering hostility.[13]   Nevertheless, they appear to be
intelligent, and to have naturally pleasant dispositions. The
men are tall, erect, and finely proportioned. Their features are
inclined to European regularity; their eyes large, shaded by long
lashes, and surrounded by circles of blue tint that add to their
apparent size. The apron or breech-cloth for men, and a short
petticoat made of strips of the inner bark of the cotton-wood for
women, are the only articles of dress deemed indispensable.
But many of the females have long robes or cloaks of furs.
The young girls wear beads. When married, their chins are
tattooed with vertical blue lines, and they wear a necklace with
a single sea-shell in front, curiously wrought. These shells are
very ancient, and are esteemed of great value. A few were in
camp to-day, mounted on spirited horses. They scrupulously
avoided all superfluous clothing, but were neatly painted and
decked in their most fashionable ornaments. Their bodies and
limbs were tinted and oiled so as to appear like well-polished
mahogany. Dandies paint their faces perfectly black. Warriors
add a streak of red across the forehead, nose, and chin. Their
ornaments consist of leather bracelets, trimmed with bright
buttons, and worn upon the left arm; a kind of tunic made of a
buckskin fringe hanging over the shoulders; beautiful eagles'
feathers, called "sormeh," sometimes white, sometimes of a
crimson tint, tied to a lock of hair, and floating from the top of
the head; and, finally, strings of wampum, made of circular
pieces of shell with holes in the centre, by which they are
strung, often several yards in length, and worn in coils about
the neck. These shell beads, which they call "pook," are their

---

[13] Antonine Leroux, the French-Canadian who also guided Gunnison, Bartlett and Beale, and who
had, in fact, been an outstanding guide and scout in the Southwest for approximately thirty years,
was probably referring to the hostilities encountered by the fur-trappers. He had also served as a
guide to Sitgreaves, and could therefore have recollected the troubles inflicted by the Indians during
this earlier venture. Foreman (1941:10-13) cites Leroux as a very great source of dependence for
Lt. Whipple. (Capt. Sitgreaves had also depended on Leroux's services a great deal.)

substitute for money, and the wealth of the individual is estimated by the amount he possesses. Among the Cuchans, in 1852, a foot in length was worth the value of a horse. Divisions to that amount are made by the insertion of blue stones, such as by Coronado and Alarcon were called turkoises, and are now found among the ancient Indian ruins. Frequently blue beads are substituted for the more valuable stones. Turkoises and bone ornaments are also worn by chiefs, suspended from the nose. All the men of the Mojaves, Cuchans, and Maricopas have the cartilage of the nose bored, but none except men of note wear the pendant. They have also two holes bored in the rim of the ear, from which hang strings of small beads. Infants especially are decorated in this last fashion, having absolutely nothing besides upon their persons. Among the articles seen, which may be ranked as curiosities, were a bronzed medal, a clay image, and a net for catching rabbits. The former being of Spanish origin, was probably taken from the mission of San Pablo, which was founded by Father Pedro Fort[14] at the junction of Rio Gila with the Colorado in 1780, and destroyed by the Indians the same year. It represents a cardinal, with an image of the sun and a motto. The clay image is about six inches in length, and reminds one of South American idols, such as are represented by Prescott, Ewbank, and others. The formation of the eyes, nose, and mouth indicates some imitative skill. Its body terminates without legs or feet.

Notwithstanding the great numbers of Indians in camp, no village is seen near us. But we are upon a lagoon some distance from the river, and the valley is so wide that huts upon either bank would be invisible from our present position. Those who were in camp yesterday were of Captain Manuel's band. The present party is that of the chief Francisco, and we are told that there are three other chiefs, of equal importance, that will meet us as we advance. Towards evening the greater part of the Indians left for their homes. Francisco and a few of his friends remained, and being hungry, asked for a sheep, which was given them (Whipple 1856:112-115).

On their third day in Mojave country, Whipple's men surveyed the fertile, farm-dotted Mojave land on the eastern side of the Colorado

---

[14] This missionary's name is not "Fort", as it appears here, but rather "Font".

River and then encamped on a sandy beach for the night (Camp 1923:133). From this spot they planned to cross the river, survey the land occupied by the populous Mojave villages (present-day Needles) and head westward to find the Mojave River and a possible railroad route across the Mojave Desert. They had now spent three days in Mojave country with nary an "unfortunate incident" with the Indians.

All day (February 27), they struggled with the river whose currents upturned their improvised barge, hurled precious cargo into the water, and tangled men and small animals into the ropelines. Crossing the Colorado posed two supreme tests, one to the Mojaves, one to the white men. The Mojaves passed their friendship test by zestfully helping the white men all day long to retrieve their floating cargo and drowning sheep.[15] Whipple passed a supreme test when he stopped work at a hectic time to hold a formal council with a chief who appeared with his retinue. This capstone of courtesy won the chief's *ahotka* (good), a pronouncement with weight among his people.

The dramatic episode of crossing the Colorado River, vulnerable to attack but befriended instead, was a high point in Whipple's experiences with the Mojaves, but it was not the climax. While the white men in Camp 134 sorted their water-soaked paraphernalia, discarding this and salvaging that, the Mojaves held a National Council. No one knows where, when, or for how long, but the results were momentous symbols of trust. In National Council, the Mojaves took these official actions: (1) They approved a proposed plan for a road for travel and trade through their country; (2) they decided to show Whipple their secret trail to the ocean where there was water and grass; (3) and they elected a high-ranking Mojave to guide the expedition over the route. The chiefs jointly conveyed these decisions to Whipple on his last day in the Mojave Valley, with their message to the great Chief of the United States. They presented the guide, who was, says Whipple, "our old friend, a subchief named *Cairook*." *Cairook* took with him the young subchief *Iretaba*.

Whipple's narrative of these experiences in the Mojave Valley follows from the point where we left him on the preceding page.

> February 26, Camp 133. With the chief Francisco for guide, and José for interpreter, preceded and followed by great crowds of Indians, we continued our survey up the magnificent valley of the Mojaves. The soil, for miles from the river, seemed of exceeding fertility, and was sprinkled with patches

---

[15]"They were honest. They returned every one of the sheep that had scattered" (Stillman 1988).

of young wheat and fields of corn stubble. There were no acequias. Irrigation had not been resorted to; although, without doubt, the crops would have been benefitted thereby. We frequently passed rancherias surrounded by granaries filled with corn, mezquite beans, and tornillas. The houses are constructed for durability and warmth. They are built upon sandy soil, thirty or forty feet square; the sides, about two feet thick, of wickerwork and straw; the roofs thatched, covered with earth, and supported by a dozen cotton-wood posts. Along the interior walls are ranged large earthen pots filled with stores of corn, beans, and flour for daily use. In front is a wide shed, a sort of piazza, nearly as large as the house itself. Here they find shelter from rain and sun. Within, surrounding a small fire in the centre, they sleep, protected from the cold. But their favorite resort seems to be upon the top, where we usually could count from twenty to thirty persons, all apparently at home. Near the houses were a great number of cylindrical structures, with conical roofs, quite skillfully made of osier twigs. They were the granaries referred to above, for their surplus stores of corn and the mezquite fruit. The latter is highly saccharine, and, when ground to flour, is a favorite article of food with the Indians of the Gila and Colorado rivers. Its flavor is similar to that of pinole, and this name, taken from the Spanish, is sometimes applied to it. Among the most curious articles of household furniture noticed were the pestle and mortar for grinding flour. The latter was of granite, the cavity worn with beautiful regularity into a conical form, six inches wide at top, and from a foot to eighteen inches deep. The pestle of polished greenstone, also, was perfectly symmetrical, being oval-shaped, a foot and a half long, and four inches in central diameter. Judging from the slight difference in price between grains and flour, it would seem that the labor of grinding is esteemed of little account.

As we passed these rancherias, the women and children usually watched us from the housetops, and the young men, for a moment, suspended their sport with hoop and poles. There would then take place an animated discussion with our guide, as to whether we should follow the trail to the right or left, so as to avoid trampling upon the numerous wheat-fields. At first, only a small portion of the villagers seemed inclined to join us; but at length, rising an eminence, we looked back, and our little train appeared swelled to a grand army a mile in extent.

Having travelled about ten miles in a generally north-west course, we descended from the cultivated fields and cotton-wood groves to the sandy shore of the willow-bound river, where we encamped. There was little grass in the vicinity, and the mules were sent to browse on bushes. But soon the Indians brought bundles of green rushes, and large quantities of corn and mezquite beans, to be exchanged for shirts, pieces of red flannel, &c., so that at night the mules fared sumptuously.

The day has been warm and pleasant, and the evening clear. Astronomical observations were made, to fix the position of camp. Under the directions of Lieutenant Ives, preparations were commenced for crossing the river. An old and much worn India rubber pontoon, brought from New Mexico, was inflated, and the body of the spring-wagon fastened upon it. The vessel was then launched, and sat upon the water like a swan. The Indians were greatly disappointed, for they had hoped to ferry us across themselves, and be well paid for it. They all left camp at dark. Some think this deviation from previous custom looks ominous. But being now near to their lodges, they are doubtless only seeking warmer shelter than our inhospitable camp affords them.

February 27, Camp 134. We were favored with a clear and calm morning, and hastened to take advantage of it for crossing the river. Upon examining the pontoon, two of the cylinders were found collapsed, and the wagon-body filled with water. Lieutenant Ives, who had been the master-builder, viewed its distressed condition with considerable anxiety, but the case was not hopeless. Many of the holes in the canvass were mended, the air was replenished, and the pontoon again danced lightly upon the water. Long ropes, brought for the purpose, were attached to the two ends—one held up the bank, the other taken by swimmers across to an island about 150 yards wide, near the centre of the river. Upon either side was a channel from six to twelve feet deep, and about 500 feet wide, making the whole distance from the left to the right bank of the river nearly 500 yards. The current was at this place about three miles an hour. By letting out the cord from the main land and drawing in the other extremity, the first load passed safely across to the island. The second trial was less successful; the rapid current, and the weight of the long ropes, destroyed the equilibrium of the gondola, and upset it in the middle of the stream. During the excitement attending this misfortune, we were advised by an Indian messenger that another great chief[16] was about to pay us a visit. Turning around, we beheld quite an interesting spectacle. Approaching was the dignitary referred to, lance in hand, and apparelled in official robes. The latter consisted of a blanket thrown gracefully around him and a magnificent head-dress of black plumage covering his head and shoulders, and hanging down his back in a streamer, nearly to the ground. His pace was slow, his eyes cast downward, and his whole demeanor expressive of a formal solemnity. Upon his right hand was the interpreter, upon his left a boy acting as a page, and following was a long procession of his warriors, attended by a crowd of men, women, and children. Having arrived within fifty yards, he beckoned his people to sit down upon the ground; while, with interpreter and page, he presented himself before us. Taking from the boy a paper, he offered one of the stereotyped credentials given by Major Heintzelman at Fort Yuma. That having been pronounced "a-hot'-ka" (good), he took a seat upon the blanket spread for him, and smoked with us the pipe of peace. This done, we made the usual explanations of the object of the expedition; the wishes of our great Captain, the President of the United States; and the benefits that would result to them from opening a highway for emigrants, or a railroad, and thus creating a market for the produce of their fertile valley. The chief replied by a long and vehement speech, in which he expressed his satisfaction at the prospect of establishing a system of trade with the whites, whereby their nakedness would be clothed and their comforts increased; and promised that, not only should our mules and other property be sacred in their sight, but that they would afford us every assistance in their power to accomplish the objects of our mission. Then, after gifts of tobacco, blankets, and trinkets, had been presented, and by the chief distributed to his people, the council of state was turned into a general trading community. The Indians were decked in their most valued ornaments, and a furor possessed all of our party to obtain some trophy. Therefore trinkets and

---

[16] This was the great Mojave chieftain *humma-sick-a-hoit*, head of the Mojave government and a famed warrior, wary statesman and sagacious counselor. He was intensely nationalistic, vigilant in the defense and protection of the Mojave territory from encroachment, and was being a stickler for Mojave customs.

garments were bought and sold upon both sides; although civilization's seemed at a discount, and the relics of barbarism vastly above par. Shell beads and necklaces would be sold, perhaps, for a blanket and shirt; while a fine bow and quiver of arrows would command several of them. The Indians were shrewd, and would part with no article without a really valuable compensation. Tobacco they would accept as a gift only, and then sell it to the soldiers. There is a species of wild tobacco which grows here, and is used by the natives. I presume they prefer it to the best Havana. Vermilion, oil paints, glass and coral beads, we could scarcely give away. White cotton cloth, calico, blankets, and white porcelain beads, would have purchased probably a thousand pounds of flour, and hundreds of bushels of grain.

Fortunately, this sudden accession of visitors did not impede the busy and difficult operation of crossing the river. We left the gondola, as it was called, bottom upwards; men beneath it, entangled among boxes, and struggling for life. The revolution of the boat had been so rapid, that most of the baggage was caught by the top of the wagon body, and there suspended. The men also were supported by the same. After a desperate struggle they disentangled themselves. The boat was pulled ashore, unloaded, righted, and once more set to work. By using increased caution, we succeeded in passing to the island without further accident. To reach the western bank we had a channel to cross still more rapid and deep, and were more unfortunate even than before—our loaded barge three times casting its contents into the river. Mr. White and a little Mexican boy were nearly drowned, before the exertions of Mr. Möllhausen succeeded in extricating them from beneath the boat. The Indians, who are capable swimmers, plunged in, and aided us in saving much of the property. Many of them had brought rafts to the spot, in the hope that they might be required. These were of simple construction, being merely bundles of rushes placed side by side, and securely bound together with willow twigs. But they were light and manageable, and their owners paddled them about with considerable dexterity.

It was night when finally the great work was accomplished; the crossing of the Colorado completed, and camp formed upon the right bank. But our joy in the event was considerably tempered by the accidents that had befallen us.

Some things were lost; others wet and ruined. Our mules swam across and landed safely, a piece of good fortune that all appreciated. The sheep were brought over by our rather officious, but exceedingly useful Mojave allies. By no fault of theirs, but from bad management of the boat-rope, several sheep became entangled in the cord and were drowned. These were given to Indians, who swam out for them. Two more sheep and two blankets were awarded to the pilots of the flock. We landed upon a field of young wheat, for which the owner claimed damages; but his charge was moderate, and through the chief the matter was satisfactorily arranged.

José Maria, the fifth and last great chief of the Mojaves, here appeared with his warriors for the customary parade, and smoke, and speeches, and gifts. The whole five, Manuel, Francisco, Joachin, Oré, and José Maria, at length came in a body, desiring papers to inform succeeding parties of their civility to us. They were given, all containing warnings to afford no good cause of offence, and to be watchful.

Our gifts had now exhausted the stock for trade; large quantities of grain were in camp for sale, but when told we were too poor to buy, the Indians expressed no disappointment, but wandered from fire to fire, laughing, joking, curious but not meddlesome; trying with capital imitative tongue to learn our language, and to teach their own. Few remained in camp after sunset.

The day has been very fine; a better for our operations could not have been desired. The evening is clear, calm, and mild.

February 28, Camp 134. The mules and sheep were grazed last night in charge of a few herders several miles from camp. Our Indian neighbors did not disturb them.

To-day we have remained in camp, endeavoring to remedy yesterday's misfortunes, by drying the books and papers, and cleaning and readjusting the instruments. Some of the less valuable of the latter, found ruined, were condemned and abandoned. To a great portion of the stationery and books of reference was awarded the same fate. All of the straps belonging to the pack-saddles were missing, and search for them, by diving in the river, was in vain. Fortunately, the spring-wagon, with odometers, and sufficient instruments for surveying and astronomical purposes, reached the shore in safety, and none of the field-notes nor scientific collections were injured or lost.

Indians all day have been numerous in camp. They have not the habit of begging; but each one comes supplied with a bag of meal, or a basket of corn, which he desires to trade for cast-off clothing.

March 1, Camp 135. The saved portion of our property having been packed, we moved on, slightly west of north, three miles, and encamped upon a long lagoon or bayou of the river, the low banks of which were covered with tall rushes. We were attended, as usual, by a train of Mojaves, and the camp became to them a scene of festivity. The chief Francisco came in without parade, and condescended to take a smoke, and looked pleased without presents. It is but just to remark, that no one of the chiefs reserved for himself any of the ceremonial gifts. They were looked upon in a national light, to be received only to distribute among the people.

There was no trading to-day, except now and then by individuals, to obtain corn for a favorite riding-mule, or some curiosity of Indian dress and manufacture. Our stock of blankets and shirts was so far reduced as to compel us to endeavor to drive hard bargains; but the Mojaves were more than a match for us. They were cool and determined, and had a fixed value for our things as well as for their own. We were obliged to pay their prices, or lose the trade. A bivalve shell, curiously carved, and suspended from the neck as a sort of charm, cost a fine blanket. So great was the regret, even then, for having parted with it, that the friends of the woman who sold it would have given seven-fold to have had it restored. Other women, possessing the same ancient relics, clung fondly to them; and as the men were particularly resolute that they should do so, it seems probably that they may have been wedding presents. Strings of small sea-shells, much prettier than the last, were easily obtained for a dollar. They have suddenly learned the value of money. In order to facilitate this knowledge, we have made a point of taking the few shillings they have offered in trade; giving shirts, and such articles as they desired, in exchange.

Generosity is not a distinguishing trait in Indian character. Instances of hospitality, however, have sometimes been noticed. The Cuchans are evidently welcomed by Mojaves wherever they go. The Pinal Lenas, when we were with them two years since, seeing us without an escort, nearly defenceless, and with a scanty allowance of provisions, generously gave us, from their winter's store of food, pine nuts and mezcal. Similar examples could be cited from most of the tribes we have met.

Every day these Indians have passed with us has been like a holiday fair, and never did people seem to enjoy such occasions more than the Mojaves have done. They have been gay and joyous, singing, laughing, talking, and learning English words, which they readily and perfectly pronounce. Everything that seems new or curious they examine with undisguised delight. This evening a greater number than usual remained in camp. Placing confidence in our good intentions and kindness, all reserve was laid aside. Tawny forms could be seen flitting from one camp-fire to another, or seated around a blaze of light, their bright eyes and pearly teeth glistening with emotions of pleasure. They exhibited Indian character in a new phase, giving an insight into the domestic amusements which are probably practiced around their firesides at home. Mingling among the soldiers and Mexicans, they were interested in games and puzzles with strings, and some of their own suggestions were quite curious.

The chiefs came to-day with the interpreter to say that a national council had been held, at which they approved of the plan for opening a road to travellers through the Mojave country. They knew that upon the trail usually travelled by the Pai-Utes towards California the springs of water were small, and insufficient for our train; that on the journey our mules therefore would perish from thirst, and the expedition fail. Hence they had selected a good man, who knew the country well, and determined to send him to guide us by another route, where sufficient water and grass could be found. They wished us to report favorably to our great chief, in order that he might send many more of his people to pass this way, and bring clothing and utensils to trade for the produce of their fields.

The guide presented was our old friend, a sub-chief called "Cai-rook," who had so successfully conducted the instrument wagon and the surveyors around the mountain spur which intersected the Colorado valley between the country of the Chemehuevis and that of the Mojave Indians. He professes his willingness to accompany us to the junction of the Mormon road with the Mojave river. Pointing to the position which the sun would have in the sky at the commencement and end of each march, and closing a finger to mark each day, he clearly described the route, and the time it would require to perform the journey. He also made a trace of it upon the ground, laying down the position of each stream and spring, and stating whether much or little water would be found at the several points. To different persons his explanation was the same, and would never admit the possibility of encountering more or less obstacles than he had at first denoted. The price of his services was to consist of a blue blanket, a Mexican serape, a short, and a few strings of white beads. At his request a dragoon overcoat was added. The serape was presented at once. The remaining articles were to be given at the conclusion of his services. Cairook then left camp, promising to be with us early on the morrow (Whipple 1856:115-119).

Whipple's expedition broke camp on March 2, 1854 and, guided by *Cairook*, headed out of the Mojave Valley,[17] trailed by Mojave well-wishers, while behind them smoke messages along the river signalled their departure.

The next long stretch of Whipple's itinerary can be traced, approximately, by today's Santa Fe Railway running west from Needles through Barstow and San Bernardino to Los Angeles, California. Modern engineering has made many cut-offs but vestiges of the old road can be seen yet.[18]

---

[17]"The Mojaves told them, 'You'll die of thirst; follow the mountains. Go to the mountains. The mountains hold water.' That's why they followed the mountains" (Stillman 1988).

[18]"[The railroad] went through the mountains in that early time. But later when the white people learned how to pump water from underground water, they bottled that water, [and the railroad was moved to where] the Santa Fe rails are now laid. But in those early times, our people used the rock mountain [route] because there were springs" (Stillman 1988). Stillman went on to say that the first well was at the end of "what's now called the Dead Mountains. . . we have a different name for them. That's near the Nevada line, as [the trail] crosses the river from Fort Mojave—at the end there. That's the first well, and the second well is what we know as Paiute [springs], and then on to the [next]. We call [the first well] '*higo*,' meaning 'white.' Well, I don't know what the original [meaning] was, but that's what we called the white people later" (1988).

This was the old trail to the ocean used by Mojave traders "since time immemorial."[19]   Three times in recorded history, Mojaves guided foreigners over their secret trail: the priest, Francisco Garcés, during the Spanish period in the southwest; the lost trapper and trailblazer, Jedediah Smith, during the Mexican period; and now Whipple and Ives, U. S. Topographical Engineers. The surveyors found that the railroad route could be built along this trail from the Colorado River to the Mormon Road.

By 1855, the War Department knew that a railroad route could be built along the thirty-fifth parallel from the Mississippi River to the Pacific Ocean.

Whipple, ruminating on the Mojaves, wrote:

> There is no doubt that, before many years pass away, a great change will take place in their country. The advancing tide of emigration will soon take possession of it and, unless the strong arm of the government protects them, the native population will be driven to the mountains or be exterminated (Whipple 1856:124).

To the Mojaves, Whipple's expedition presaged a better time ahead. To them it was the opening of the great trade route through their country whereon white men, like Whipple and his men, would travel and trade. Mojave hopes were high, their spirits refreshed, and their bodies were bedecked with foreign imports—strips of blankets, calico, coats, shirts, hats, britches, and blue and white beads galore—symbols of a new day and a new friendship.

---

[19] The phrase—"since time immemorial"—refers to an old Mojave expression that is used to designate periods of time long ago, almost of a primordial nature.

CHAPTER V:
BEALE'S SURVEY FOR A WAGON ROAD

Three years elapsed between Whipple's exit from the Mojave Valley and the appearance of the next War Department expedition. Then, in the autumn of 1857, an expedition headed by Edward Fitzgerald Beale worked its way over the route from Zuni toward the Colorado River. Stopping here to build a culvert, here and there to dislodge rocks and remove brush, the party headed westward, endeavoring to make a road over which wagon wheels could go.

The significance of the expedition varied according to the point of view held by each of the several groups affected by it. To the Mojaves, the coming of this 1857-58 expedition was a sign of the fulfillment of their agreement with Lieutenant Whipple that the United States would build a trade route through their country for the mutual benefit of both peoples (Whipple 1856:117). To the War Department, the Beale mission meant the opening of a road which could be used the year around for the military protection of the West, as well as the testing of a new means of military transportation—the camel.[1]

Congress, for its part, justified the appropriation of funds for the venture on the grounds that the road would provide a route for travel while the problems involved in building railroads were being threshed out.

The man appointed to command this expedition, Edward Fitzgerald Beale, Superintendent of Indian Affairs in California, was no

---

[1]This reference is to Beale's orders, to his mission. See Floyd 1858.

novice in the west. As a young naval officer, Beale had distinguished himself for heroism in line duty on the Pacific Coast during the Mexican War (Bonsal 1912:26-27). He had been "the man of the hour" when, in 1848 he made a solo, record-breaking trip from California to Washington, D.C. via Mexico, bringing gold to apprise the government of California's rich strike (1912:42-63). He had resigned his naval career to become a land-lubber-pathfinder, trekking across country wilderness with cool resourcefulness to promote transcontinental roads for emigrant travel, and working prodigiously to protect Indians by placing them upon self-sustaining reservations guarded against white men's aggression.[2]

It is doubtful that any man in the United States could boast of greater east-west mileage than Beale, or of half his independence, coolness, and dangerous experiences. His acumen in Indian affairs had netted him the superintendency of Indian Affairs in California; his foresight had netted him an estate in California said to be about half the size of Rhode Island; his boundless energy and courage had netted him popular acclaim. In addition, his continuous barrage on the War Department had placed him in the forefront in drumming up an interest in camels as an effective means of military transportation in the West. It so happened that Jefferson Davis, as a Senator, and later as Secretary of War, shared Beale's views on camels. It was Davis who had obtained Congressional appropriations to import camels from the Far East (1912:255). About eighty of the animals, kept mainly in Texas, were inherited by his successor in office. To the new Secretary of War, John B. Floyd, Beale seemed well-tailored for the new double-duty assignment.

Beale's mission for the War Department, therefore, was to superintend the survey of a wagon road from Fort Defiance to the Colorado River, and while he was at it, to test the efficiency of camels as a means of military transportation (Beale 1858:38). An enthusiast for both projects, Beale picked up his camels, mules, wagons and men in San Antonio, Texas on June 25, 1857, and headed for Fort Defiance, New Mexico, his official starting point. Since the fort was about thirty miles above the proposed wagon route, Beale sent his outfit directly to the Zuni villages where he was to buy corn. From there he rode with two other horsemen up to Fort Defiance to pick up his military escort and to fulfill to the letter his official orders from the War Department.

The expedition left the Zuni villages on August 31, 1857 (Beale 1858:46). It was, by any description, a curious mixture of men, animals, and wagons—United States surveyors and soldiers, a Mexican guide and

---

[2]A close scrutiny of the documentary evidence suggests that the motive for Beale's efforts to get Indians on reservations was probably as much to move them off lands that he and others wanted for themselves as to protect the Indians.

Mexican herders, Greek and Turkish camel drivers, a goodly quota of horses and mules, twenty-five camels, and about three hundred fifty sheep, as meat on the hoof (1858:67).

Beale's idea of surveying a wagon route was to leave tracks and campsites that could be used immediately by wagon trains, and to accompany his report to the War Department with a detailed description of the route which would serve as an emigrant's guide. Through some stretches of country he was able to take his wagons, mules and camels across hard ground that made a natural dirt road. Through others he camped briefly to cut through brush and to make crude fills for his wagons. He found some exasperating geographic road blocks, such as Canyon Diablo, so named by Whipple because of its precipitous walls and deep abyss. Beale termed this gaping canyon "a mere chasm in a plain," which cost him a two-day detour.

Beale visualized dams (canyons which could catch and hold bountiful waters for passers through) where dams were not. He found the country along the thirty-fifth parallel to have salubrious climate, unexcelled beauty, bountiful game, luxuriant grass, a few timid Indians, picturesque cliffs, and generous valleys that would be a paradise for stock. Of the Indians he wrote, "Poor creatures! Their time will come soon enough for extermination when the merits of this road are made known, and it becomes, as it most assuredly will, the thoroughfare to the Pacific."

"Up at three o'clock, off at five"[3] epitomized Beale's pattern of work as his train moved across what he felt to be the best potential route of travel in the West. On October 13, the expedition wearied its way through geographic hardships and camped in the mountains overlooking the Colorado River. Here the men lighted fire-signals to tell the Mojaves that they were advancing, and wanted to trade.

In camp on the night of October 18, Beale wrote a long letter to the Secretary of War.

> Sir: I have the honor to report my arrival in California, after a journey of forty-eight days. It gives me great pleasure to inform you that we have met with the most complete success in our exploration for a wagon road from New Mexico to this State . . . (Beale 1858:72).

After a brief recapitulation of his exploration from Zuni to the Colorado, Beale enumerated the advantages of the route:

---

[3]"Up at four, off at five", "up at 4, off at 5 1/2", etc., appears throughout Beale's reports, reflecting his minuteness of detail, his systematic way of going about things.

It is the shortest from our western frontier by 300 miles, being nearly directly west. It is the most level: our wagons only double-teaming once in the entire distance, and that at a short hill, and over a surface heretofore unbroken by wheels or trail of any kind. It is well watered: our greatest distance without water at any time being about twenty miles. It is well timbered, and in many places the growth is far beyond that of any part of the world I have ever seen. It is temperate in climate, passing for the most part over an elevated region. It is salubrious: not one of our party requiring the slightest medical attendance from the time of our leaving to our arrival. It is well grassed; my command never having made a bad grass camp during the entire distance, until near the Colorado. It crosses the great desert (which must be crossed by any road to California) at its narrowest point. It passes through the country abounding in game, and but little infested with Indians. On the entire road, until our arrival at the Mojave villages, we did not see, in all, over a dozen Indians, and those of a timid and inoffensive character. At the point of the crossing of the Colorado, grain, vegetables, and breadstuffs may be obtained in any quantity from the Indians, who cultivate extensively, though rudely, the fertile bottom lands of the Colorado. It is passable alike in winter and summer . . . (Beale 1858:73-76).[4]

After a eulogy on the camels, Beale described how he got his camels across the river. A report that camels could not swim caused some anxiety.

However, . . . I determined to test the truth of the statement which I had seen in relation to that fact. The first one (camel) brought down to the river's edge refused to take the water. Anxious, but not discouraged, I ordered another one to be brought, one of our largest and finest; and only those who have felt so much anxiety for the success of an experiment can imagine my relief on seeing it take to the water and swim boldly across the rapidly flowing river. We then tied them, one to the saddle of another, and, without the slightest difficulty, in a short time swam them all to the opposite side in gangs, five in a gang; to my delight, they not only swam with

---

[4]The route did become an emigrant road. In a sense, it still is one, for it parallels the path of Old Highway 66.

ease, but with apparently more strength than horses or mules. One of them, heading up stream, swam a considerable distance against the current, and all landed in safety on the other side (Beale 1858:1).

Beale's journal and his letter of October 18th to the Secretary of War did not mention any difficulties or threatened difficulties with the Mojaves at the Colorado River. But Humphrey Stacey, one of Beale's assistants, wrote in his journal on October 18 that the Mojaves stopped Beale from going down the river (Stacey 1929:2-3). However, the men, ready for a fight, met many Indians and camped by the river. (The Indians apparently made no move to stop the armed men.) Stacey, in his journal of October 19, wrote that the men were in the water all day transporting baggage. "Expecting a fight all day. Men in readiness. Attitude of the Indians very precarious and not at all permanent" (1929:4). On the following day, Indians "rather better disposed" came into camp to trade.

It can be inferred that the Mojaves had slight grounds for admiring the camels–these creatures with long necks and big mouths that could reach the topmost boughs of the mesquite trees and tear off branches. The mesquite, which grew plentifully in the valley, was a staple food provided by *Mutivillya*. The thorny, prickly pear provided fruit for the tribe. Animals that destroyed orchards were not to the Mojaves' liking.[5]

---

[5]Stillman's present-day comment on Beale may reflect the general attitude of her nineteenth century forebears on Beale, if not on his camels: Beale, she says, "came right in and looked like he owned the place, and didn't bother to talk to anybody, or ask if he might cross or anything. That's what our people didn't like about Beale. He acted as though he owned the whole world."

"Beale was like Sitgreaves in that he wanted nothing to do with the Mojave. He went right through. The Mojaves did nothing to him. They wanted to be friends, but he did not respond. He crossed right in the middle of their land and their river. Now it's everybody's river. They're taking the water everywhere now. Just a little stream now. The Colorado was a mighty river when I was a child. All the birds have disappeared—the water birds. In the fall they used to have a lot of different kinds of Canadian geese and others. Now not a one. Everything's disappeared, even the vegetation—the wild plants we had. The fish are all gone, too. We had five kinds at one time, but now they plant some kind of things—the kind that other people like" (1989).

CHAPTER VI: THE MORMONS AND BEALE

Beale's crossing of the Colorado River in October, 1857, occurred during a time when the Mojaves were becoming puzzled and alarmed by strange doings above their northern border among the Paiutes, the Utes and the Mormons, as well as by strange doings below their southern border around Fort Yuma.[1] By 1857-58, the long, smoldering conflict between the Mormons in the Utah Territory and the United States threatened to burst into a shooting war that would involve both whites and Indians.[2]

---

[1] In the years 1857 and 1858, the West was troubled with Latter Day Saint (Mormon) and Indian warfare. In 1847, the first Mormons had arrived in their new home, which they named Deseret (and the United States soon renamed Utah) while this territory was still within the jurisdiction of Mexico. By 1857, the Mormons had planted a colony across the Mojave Desert, near San Bernardino, had another settlement in Carson Valley, and were making ingratiating advances among the Indian tribes along the Colorado River. Details of these advances can be found in Ives 1861:44, 88-89. The "strange doings" around Ft. Yuma consisted of the mysterious competition, to be referred to again later in the text, displayed by Lt. Ives and Capt. George Alonzo Johnson in their separate efforts at exploring Colorado.

[2] In September 1850, Congress approved the organization of the Utah Territory, and the President appointed its civil officers. Brigham Young, the civil and religious leader of the Mormons, was confirmed as the first governor and ex-officio Superintendent of Indian Affairs. After a long series of alleged offenses against civil officers (all but two of the Indian agents were forced to leave the Territory for their personal safety), the United States government appointed a new staff of civil officers, including the governor, and sent with them a small military escort for their protection. Upon learning of this move, the Utah Territory broke into open insurrection, which was not terminated until June 1858. For President Buchanan's own view of this problem see Buchanan 1858:23-26. This address has also been reproduced in Richardson 1898. See also U. S. Department of War 1860 II:6-15.

During the last half of 1857, the Mormons made an exodus from their prosperous, outlying farms and settlements in order to join their brethren in Salt Lake City for the purpose of defending Zion. The long wagon trains of men, women, and children all bound toward the same point puzzled the Indians. The Mormon road through Las Vegas, which angled above the North Mojave country, crawled with wagons all going to Salt Lake. From mid-June until mid-November, long columns of United States troops and heavy army supply trains moved across country toward a rendezvous preparatory to a concerted drive into Utah Territory. The Expedition of Utah, under the command of Brevet Brigadier Albert Sidney Johnston, bivouacked under winter snows within marching distance of Salt Lake City, ready for a showdown with defiant Brigham Young, come fair weather (Buchanan 1858:23-26).

Military intelligence of the United States Army had a creditable amount of information that the Mormons were stirring trouble among the Indians. Such departmental commanders as General Garland of the Department of New Mexico, and General Clarke of the Department of the Pacific, foresaw formidable trouble should the Indians wage an all-out war, abetted by or in alliance with the Mormons.[3]

Focus was on the Colorado and the Mojaves.

The Mojaves, in their secluded homeland, had escaped the military and emigrant travel that finally caused Fort Yuma to be established on the Colorado River among their old friends and allies, the Quechans.

But now, unfortunately, the navigability of the Colorado had military value for both the United States and the Mormons in Utah Territory. The fact that this great river cut its way through Mojave country from north to south, with the Mojaves living peacefully along its banks, concerned each side less than its own military strategy.

---

[3] On January 1, 1858, General N. S. Clarke, commanding the Department of the Pacific, informed the General-in-chief of the Army that he had received from different sources information that the Mormons were endeavoring to incite Indian tribes in Washington Territory and in California to hostilities against the United States. "If these things are true," he wrote, "and I credit them, temporary success on the part of the Mormons may be a signal for an Indian war extending along our whole frontier" (Clarke 1858:335-36).

On January 24 and 31, and March 1 and 13, 1858, General John Garland, commanding the Department of New Mexico, sent to Colonel A. S. Johnston, commanding the Utah expedition, information that the Mormons, through the Utes, were trying to persuade the Navajos to hostilities (Garland 1858:281-82, 287).

Also, on May 6, 1858, Colonel Skeptve, commanding Fort Walla Walla, Washington Territory, was attacked by a war party of Spokanes, Pelouses, Couer d'Alenes, Yakimas, and others (U. S. Department of War 1858 II:341-48).

Military intelligence of the Mojaves—by which is meant their scouting and courier systems—had a creditable amount of conflicting information about the motives and activities of both the United States and the Mormons. From the Mojaves' standpoint, the question of which outsider was right and which was wrong in this struggle was of less consequence than the fact that they were caught in the middle, not knowing whom to believe, and unable to do as they had done in pre-white days—i.e., maintain a closed-door policy, guard their borders, and if need be, polish their war clubs and arrows and enlist aid from their friends and allies, the Quechans.

It so happened during this bewildering time that within the first two months of 1858, three United States expeditions crossed Mojave country: Beale came back again to cross the river eastbound with his camels; and two steamboats came up the river and went back down—Captain Johnson, with his steamboat the *General Jesup*, and Lieutenant Ives with his steamer the *Explorer*. All had military escorts. Meanwhile, Mormons were penetrating Mojave country from the north, both by foot and by horseback.

Six weeks after Beale crossed the Colorado among grim-faced Mojaves, Lieutenant Joseph C. Ives, previously a member of the Whipple expedition, and part of his command debarked on November 30, 1857 (Ives 1861:26) from the schooner *Monterey* at the mouth of the Colorado, unloading what Ives called "an awkward mass of freight" (1861:21)—the makings of a steamboat. Ives' mission for the War Department was to explore the navigability of the Colorado River. He was to organize a base of operations, and from it supply a military escort.

Ives' exploratory plans at this critical time caused a commotion among Indian tribes on the Colorado River and among the Mormons, both in Utah Territory and around Fort Yuma. His commission was fraught with danger and with military urgency. It was also filigreed with political questions, among which was why go to the expense of building a steamboat in the East and shipping it in parts to be reassembled at the mouth of the Colorado. This question took on added puzzlement, especially since such a steamboat as the *General Jesup*, owned by Captain George Alonzo Johnson, was operating as far up the river as Fort Yuma and could have been obtained at less cost through contract. There were those who felt that the experienced Captain Johnson had been bypassed for a young lieutenant out to make a name for himself.[4] One allegation was that the expedition of Lieutenant Ives was a political plum,

---

[4] A leader in holding this point of view was no other than Captain Johnson himself (Hayes n.d.:585 as quoted from Woodward 1955:74).

fallen his way because of his affiliation with the family of the Secretary of War.[5]

The *Explorer*, as the little steamboat was called, was constructed in Philadelphia, tested on the Delaware, and then taken apart and shipped from New York to San Francisco via the Isthmus of Panama. Next, the "awkward mass of freight" was shipped to the mouth of the Colorado River. Here, at Robinson's Landing, Lieutenant Ives, A. J. Carroll, engineer and builder of the *Explorer*, and a crew of men spent a feverish month assembling the craft and testing its performance. These activities attracted curious visitors—among them the Cocopah Indians, who had been enemies of the Mojave and the Quechan Indians "beyond the span of memory" (Ives 1861:34), and Captain George Alonzo Johnson, who viewed the proceedings with jaundiced eyes. Captain Johnson had no notion of permitting a greenhorn on the river to explore its navigability with a little fifty-foot steamer while he sat by with a substantial steamboat twice as long and much more seasoned and river-worthy. He promptly fitted the *General Jesup* for an exploration as far up the Colorado as a steamboat could go before Ives could get his *Explorer* into the water, and requested a detachment of troops from the fort as military escort (Woodward 1955:70). His proposed venture was a windfall to the temporary commander at Fort Yuma, Lieutenant William A. Winder. This side issue of politics and rivalry would be extraneous to Mojave history except that the unprecedented voyage of the *General Jesup* up the river above Yuma, followed shortly by the *Explorer*, caused reverberations of alarm and suspicion among the river tribes.

Lieutenant Winder had received dispatches from General Clarke alerting him to the eminence of a war in the Utah territory, and to reports of Mormon infiltration among the Mojaves. Foreseeing a likelihood of Fort Yuma becoming a supply base in the looming action against the Mormons, Winder sent Lieutenant James A. White with a detachment of troops as military escort to the *General Jesup* with instructions to obtain information about "the real state of the Mojaves, also whether or not the Colorado River is navigable for steamboats" (Winder 1857). One shining feature behind this arrangement was Captain Johnson's offer to conduct White's party free of charge.

Accordingly, on December 31, one week before Ives arrived at Fort Yuma, Captain Johnson triumphantly nosed his *General Jesup* out

---

[5] This charge was also made by Captain Johnson, five years after the affair, in a conversation with Judge Benjamin Hayes. Johnson allegedly told Hayes that the reason Ives received the appropriation was that the Lieutenant was married to a niece of the Secretary of War (Hayes n.d.:585 in Woodward 1955:70).

of Yuma and wrestled it up the tortuous Colorado River. Aboard were Lieutenant White with his soldiers and fifteen well-armed men, among them Pauline Weaver, a beaver trapper (Woodward 1955:83). The big steamboat entered Mojave country below Bill William's Fork, made its way through the Mojave Canyon, through the Mojave Valley up to Cottonwood Island in northern Mojave country, poked around there, and then came back down the river. On this trip Captain Johnson and Lieutenant White discovered that the Colorado was navigable by steamboats as far upstream as Cottonwood Island. The Mojaves discovered, much to their consternation, that white men's steamboats could navigate the river from the southernmost part of their holdings to their northernmost settlements. They were thus alerted to a new threat. They were vulnerable to attack by way of the river!

Lieutenant White found out in the course of the trip that the Mormons had indeed sowed alarm and suspicion among the Mojaves; that the Mojaves were dubious of the intentions of the United States, and also apprehensive of the intentions of the Mormons (White 1858). He explained to Mojave chiefs, as best he could, the causes of the conflict between the United States and the Mormons, and received from them assurance that they would remain loyal to the United States. In case of open warfare, the Mojaves would side with the United States, although they feared reprisals from the Mormons. Lieutenant White felt that his reassurance and promises to the Mojaves relieved any animosities they might have harbored against the United States. Describing them in his report to Lieutenant Winder, he stated:

> In regard to the Mojaves, they met us with such marked friendship and cordiality, both sexes and all ages assembling by hundreds upon the banks as we passed through their valley; exhibiting no indication of hostility, no apprehension of evil design on our part and apparently conscious of deserving none (White 1858, quoted in Woodward 1955:103).

Whatever assurance the Mojaves may have felt was undermined by what seemed to be a rendezvous between the *General Jesup* and Beale's expedition. The *General Jesup*, mission accomplished, hove to and anchored near "Beale's Crossing" on January 22, 1858. Beale, with his expedition, was within less than a day's march of "Beale's Crossing", eastward bound via the "Surveyor's Trail"—the old Indian trail over which Cairook and Iretaba had guided Whipple and Ives. His expedition was headed for the river-crossing, to retrace in winter the route to Zuni

along the 35th parallel that had been surveyed for a wagon road during
the summer and fall months of 1857.

On January 22, 1858, Beale and his camels, accompanied by an
escort of sixty dragoons from Fort Tejon, reappeared at the banks of the
Colorado opposite the site where the *General Jesup* lay. Beale's journal
tells what happened, as he saw it.

Saturday, January 23, 1858. We reached the Colorado
River early in the morning, having encamped in a rainstorm the
night previous a few miles from it. Shortly after leaving camp,
my clerk, F. E. Kerlin, who with two of my party had been
despatched the day previous in order to have my boat ready for
crossing, was seen returning. Various surmises were immediately started as to the cause, and as soon as he was within
speaking distance he was questioned eagerly for the news. He
gave us a joyful surprise by the information that the steamer
General Jesup, Captain Johnson, was at the crossing waiting to
convey us to the opposite side. It is difficult to conceive the
varied emotions with which this news was received. Here, in
a wild, almost unknown country, inhabited only by savages, the
great river of the west, hitherto declared unnavigable, had, for
the first time, borne upon its bosom that emblem of civilization,
a steamer. The enterprise of a private citizen had been
rewarded by success, for the future was to lend its aid in the
settlement of our vast western territory. But alas! for the poor
Indians living on its banks and rich meadow lands. The rapid
current which washes its shores will hardly pass more rapidly
away. The steam whistle of the *General Jesup* sounded the
death knell of the river race.

Accompanying Captain Johnson, was Lieutenant White,
of the United States army, and fifteen soldiers as an escort,
which, with as many rugged mountain men, and the steamer as
a fort, made a dangerous party to meddle with.

In a few minutes after our arrival the steamer came
alongside the bank, and our party was transported at once, with
all our baggage, to the other side. We then swam the mules
over, and bidding Captain Johnson good-bye, he was soon
steaming down the river towards Fort Yuma, three hundred and
fifty miles below. I confess I felt jealous of his achievement,
and it is to be hoped the government will substantially reward
the enterprising spirit which prompted a citizen, at his own risk

and at great hazard, to undertake so perilous and uncertain an
expedition.

I had brought the camels with me, and as they stood on
the bank, surrounded by hundreds of wild unclad savages, and
mixed with these the dragoons of my escort and the steamer
slowly revolving her wheels preparatory to a start, it was a
curious and interesting picture (Beale, cited in Casebier
1975:69-70).

Beale's return trip over the route from the Colorado River to Fort
Defiance during January and February confirmed his conviction that this
route along the 35th parallel was practicable the year around. Moreover,
his expedition experienced no hostilities from Indians other than shouts
and yells from the Hualapais, made a safe distance from gun fire.

On February 21, a few miles from his terminal, Fort Defiance, he
wrote in his journal:

A year in the wilderness has ended! During this time
I have conducted my party from the Gulf of Mexico to the
shores of the Pacific Ocean, and back again to the eastern
terminus of the road, through a country for a great part entirely
unknown, and inhabited by hostile Indians, without the loss of
a man. I have tested the value of camels, marked a new road
to the Pacific, and traveled 4000 miles without an accident
(Beale 1858:86-87).

In his report and his recommendations to the Secretary of War,
dated April 26, 1858, Beale further stated,

I presume there can be no further question as to the
practicability of the country near the thirty-fifth parallel for a
wagon road, since Aubrey, Whipple, and myself, have all
traveled it successfully with wagons, neither of us in precisely
the same line, and yet through very much the same country
(Beale 1858:2).

At the conclusion of his report, Beale wrote:

I regard the establishment of a military post on the
Colorado river as an indispensable necessity for the emigrant
over this road; for, although the Indians, living in the rich
meadow lands, are agricultural, and consequently peaceable,

they are very numerous, so much so that we counted 800 men around our camp on the second day after our arrival of the banks of the river. The temptation of the scattered emigrant parties with their families, would offer too strong a temptation for the Indians to withstand (1858:3).

Whatever notions the Mojaves might have had that Beale's mission was connected with a peaceful "trade route" through their country must have been dispelled by Beale himself. He moved perfunctorily across Mojave lands without respect for Mojave protocol, camped without permission on Mojave soil, and crossed the Colorado River without Mojave sanction or assistance. The Mojaves must have sensed that the attitude of the commander of this United States expedition was that of an armed traveler who was going somewhere and brooked no interference. Coming at this particular time, his expedition lent color to what the Mormons were alleged to have told them to the effect that the United States had designs on their land.

CHAPTER VII:
ATTACK ON THE WAGON TRAIN

The fourth expedition from Zuni to the Colorado River along the thirty-fifth parallel was not a surveying expedition with a military escort, but a long wagon train of men, women, and children with nary a soldier—the first emigrants to travel the unfinished Beale road.[1] They traveled in ox-drawn prairie schooners loaded with their possessions, herding some four hundred head of cattle. Only one man in this caravan had experienced long treks across the West. He was John Udell, a 63 year-old preacher who had taken the Santa Fe Trail four times (Udell 1859:3).

Two wagon trains of emigrants from Iowa and Missouri, bound for California over the Santa Fe Trail had met by happenstance just west of Kansas City. There they decided to join forces and move together through Indian country. One train was headed by its prosperous owner, L. R. Rose, the other by Gillum Bailey, one of the joint owners of the second train. In Albuquerque, the emigrants were beguiled by the heralded advantages of the new Beale road. John Udell, with the Bailey train, appears to have been the only one who protested the change of

---

[1] The story of this emigrant-train which was attacked by Indians on the Colorado River is told by the owner of the train, L. J. Rose, and a member of the train who traveled with the Rose Party, John Udell.

Rose's eye-witness account of the attack is found in a letter that appeared in the November 9, 1859, edition of the *Missouri Republican*. The letter has since been reprinted in Cleland 1951:246-277. Udell's account of the wagon train incident can be found in Udell (1859). These are the two publications which will concern us; however, a different version of Udell's journal was published in Jefferson, Ohio, 1868, and republished in 1946 by Lyle H. Wright in the California Centennial Series.

plans, having experienced near starvation once when journeying off the beaten track among agitated Indian tribes. He wrote, "I thought it preposterous to start on so long a journey with so many women and helpless children, and so many dangers attending the attempt. A burnt child dreads fire" (Udell 1859:13).

In Albuquerque, the leaders of the wagon trains hired an "expert" guide—none other than Savedra (nicknamed Leco) who had formerly been one of Whipple's guides and who had recently served as Beale's guide. Those who recommended Savedra must not have known that Whipple had not relied on him, and that Beale had relegated him to the rear of his expedition. "We unfortunately have no guide," wrote Beale, "the wretch we employed at the urgent request and advice of everyone at Albuquerque, and at enormous wages, being the most ignorant and irresolute old ass extant" (Beale 1858:51).

The wagon trains proceeded into sparse Indian country, the Rose division leading with its carriage, four covered wagons, and about two hundred fifty head of mules, horses, oxen and cattle; the Bailey division following with its twelve covered wagons, and about two hundred heads of livestock.[2] The trains traveled separately so that the animals could find sufficient water from the springs along the way.

At Peach Springs, one hundred twelve miles east of the Colorado River, the emigrants encountered their first harassment by Indians. These Indians, termed *Cosininos,* were Yavapai and Havasupai. They stole a few animals and enjoyed playing cat-and-mouse with travelers. The harassment worsened as the trains dragged onward through Hualapai country, rounding cliffs and crossing the blazing land of the Hualapai Indians whose arrows had killed or wounded horses, cattle, and one man, rendering him unable to walk or ride horseback for two months (Cleland 1951:266-267).

In the latter part of August, 1858, a time of the year when the parched desert smolders from the unbroken heat of summer, the wagon

---

[2] The train was composed of four parties: while approaching the eastern entrance to Beale's Pass, these parties were traveling in two divisions, so that the large herd of stock might not be forced to water all at one time, thereby exhausting the smaller springs along the route.

The first division included the party of Leonard J. Rose and family; S. M. Jones and family; Alpha Brown and family; the superintendent of the train, Mr. Bentner and his family; seventeen hired-hands (herders and laborers); B. M. Savedra, the guide. The livestock consisted of 247 head of cattle, as well as twenty-one horses and mules (Cleland 1951:264-265).

The second division was composed of John Udell and wife; Tamerland Davis; John Anspach; one wagon, four oxen, two cows and one riding horse. Also, John Baily and family; Isaac Holland and family; unstated livestock (Udell 1859:4); Gillum Bailey and family; Wright Bailey and family; Joel Hedgepeth and family; Thomas Hedgepeth and family; fifteen hands, 119 head of cattle, fourteen horses and eleven wagons (Cleland 1951:264-265; Udell 1859:7).

trains reached the last range of mountains that intervened between them and the Colorado River. Under a fiery sun they entered the Black Mountains, a region that again provided no water, no grass, and held heat like a furnace. Without pausing to rest, the heavy schooners labored into Sitgreaves Pass which leads from Hualapai to Mojave country, toiling upwards and around the vaulting pinnacles that had, since time immemorial, been the watchtowers of the Mojaves[3].

Sitgreaves Pass winds tortuously over a precipitate mountain of rock, staggered by great rhyolite outcroppings, ridges and cliffs, all in gargantual volcanic disarray. (It later became Highway 66 whose serpentine edge peered dizzily straight down into the deep canyon, providing a hazardous road through the mining camps of Goldroad and Oatman.) It was up and down and around this untamed mountain[4] that, between August 25 and 27, 1858, the emigrants, together with their hundreds of complaining, thirsty cattle, toiled without rest or water (Rose 1859:18-19; Cleland 1951:267).

From the summit, the Rose party sent up hurrahs at the vision of the plentiful waters of the Colorado. From these ramparts they saw the sweep of the promised land of California. They pushed doggedly downwards through the night, breaking one wagon on the way, sustained by the hope they would reach the river at daybreak. That night, somewhere between the summit and the valley, they met their first Mojaves.

Immediately the Mojaves inquired as to the number of emigrants in the party and whether or not they planned to settle on the Colorado. Rose gave the number of his party, and also informed them that a second division was to follow. He reported that the Mojaves were "very friendly, showing us the road and performing other services unasked during the night" (Cleland 1951:266-267).

Rose then pressed his teams, men, and stock to the limit of endurance and about noon camped one mile from the river on the edge of a wood. Most of the exhausted men fell into a heavy sleep while Alpha Brown, the wagon master, herded the livestock to the river. At this time, Rose reported, the temper of the Mojaves changed—they began to kill and drive off a few cattle, cooked and ate some, and "when caught in the act would laugh and treat the matter as a huge joke" (Cleland 1951:268).

---

[3]This is now the highway to Golden Valley. It goes from Bullhead to Kingman through the Black Mountains.

[4]*Avivasqwi*, Cone Mountain.

By this time the second division had worked its way carefully over the pass and established a camp at the mouth of a canyon on the edge of the valley. Here they prepared to remain for several days to allow their women, children, and animals to rest. The young men drove all of the groggy stock down to the river that night (August 27) intending to return with the oxen and mule teams when the animals had regained strength enough to pull the heavy wagons down the precipitous road.

By the time the two separate camps had been made and the two different herds driven to the river, the Mojaves became "insolent." By nightfall, however, they had all returned to their homes. Rose noted that if his party had been attacked on that night, they would have been easy victims because only five men remained awake.

On August 29, the Rose division moved to the banks of the river. About mid-morning, a Mojave chief appeared with his retinue of warriors. The Chief wanted to know whether or not the visitors expected to settle on the Colorado. When told that the white men were going to California, Rose recalled, "He gave us a very searching look as if not half believing it" (Rose 1859). Rose then presented gifts which the Chief distributed among his followers. Apparently pleased by the gifts, the Chief gave the travellers permission to stay, and cross the river when they liked. About an hour later a second Chief appeared with his retinue. A similar exchange took place, and the Indians left. While Rose did not identify the two chiefs by name, they were undoubtedly *Cairook* and *Sickahot*.

According to Rose, at about four o'clock on the afternoon of August 30, "we moved our camp down the river about a mile, where we expected to cross it, and found excellent grass, also plenty of cottonwood for constructing a camp" (Cleland 1951:269).

The calamity that took place on August 30, 1858 marked the beginning of Bitterness Road. This episode in Mojave history has been told in different ways. Since the incident has made headlines as a "massacre," it seems only fair to quote verbatim the only eye-witness account of what took place.

Rose reported:

> Our new camp was a very pleasant one. Although the sun was very hot during the day, so much so that the horses were as wet with perspiration as if they had been in the river, yet we had a pleasant breeze from the river; the water was good and cool, and the animals were fairly "rolling in clover". The evening and night was cool and refreshing, and the next morning we felt as fresh and buoyant with hope as if we had

never lost sleep nor had any trouble. But in the calm the storm was brewing. Only two Indians made their appearance; they looked around a while and then left. About 10 o'clock A.M., we saw many Indians crossing the river, and we counted over two hundred and fifty of them. Savedra said that the Indians acted suspiciously, and I sent word to Mr. Brown to have the cattle herded near camp. Yet we had but little fear of an attack. I felt some little uneasiness on account of Mr. Bentner, who was to come that morning from the mountains.

I will explain how he came there. The first party, with Mr. Bentner, of my party, had left their wagons in the mountains, together with their families and most of their men, fearing that the animals could not stand it to the Colorado and draw a load, and had driven their animals loose, while I had all the wagons, animals and things at the river. They expected to recruit for a few days and then return with them for the wagons. Mr. Bentner, having mules, did not need so long a time for recruiting and as we would cross the river before they could, and would get some little start, and being of our company anyway, he felt anxious to be with us. I expected him early in the morning, and his not coming, as I said before, made me uneasy, and I thought I would send back to the camp we had left and possibly we might find him and family there. Dinner being nearly ready, I postponed it until after the meal. While eating dinner, one Indian made his appearance. He looked a little while and then left. One of our boys came in and said he had seen a good many Indians in the vicinity, and they had told him that a steamboat was coming up and pointed where the sun would be when the boat would land. There was quite an excitement in camp for a while, but we concluded that it was too good to be true. After dinner, two of my men left for the camp we had left the day previous, to see if they could find Bentner.

About half an hour after the men had left, the Indians came running from every quarter, out of the brush, completely surrounding the camp, and attacked us. They came within fifteen feet of our wagons and they evidently expected to find it easier work than they did, for I have no doubt they expected to massacre us. But we were well armed and the men that were in camp ready to receive them. A short time afterward, all of the men came in except two, whom I had sent to see if they could find Mr. Bentner and family; and some of the enemy being killed, they retired to a safe distance. They kept up a continued shooting of arrows for nearly two hours, and part of them having driven off all the stock except for a few near the wagons, they all left. During this time, the two men had returned and reported of having found Miss Bentner killed, her clothes torn off and her face disfigured. They knew it was unsafe for them to make any further search, and made for the camp. From this and the fact of an Indian from the other side of the river shaking some scalps at us, which he had fastened on a pole, we supposed that they had all been killed. Mr. Brown was also killed, dying in camp without a struggle. We buried him in the Colorado, and its waters will never close over a nobler or better man, for to know him was but to like him. Eleven more were wounded, who have all since recovered, or nearly so. There were about twenty-five men in the fight.

We held a consultation, and concluded, after discussing various plans, to return the way we had come. There were cattle enough left to pull one wagon, and two mules for the carriage. We loaded these with as much provision and clothing as the oxen and mules were able to pull, leaving the loads of five wagons, undisturbed, behind. We scarcely expected to make our retreat, yet every man felt disposed to sell his life as dearly as possible. We also feared that the families with the few men left in the mountains were all killed; but we made our way back undisturbed, and found them all safe. Out of near 400 head of cattle, we saved 17 head, and out of 37 horses, probably, 10. The cattle that were mine have all died on the road, from the fact of their feet giving out in again having to go over the rocky road which had previously made their feet tender; but they were in good condition otherwise, and with a few days' rest at the Colorado, and no rock on the other side, (Savedra says there is none) would have been as able to have gone on without difficulty (Rose 1859, quoted in Cleland 1951:269-277).

A significant item not contained in Rose's report was supplied by his son, L. J. Rose, Jr., in *L. J. Rose of Sunnyslope*. The last camp of the emigrants was, as previously noted, down by the river where the party expected to cross, and where there was "excellent grass, also plenty of cottonwood for constructing a camp" (Rose 1859 quoted in Cleland 1951:269). "Here also," said Rose, Jr., "were plenty of trees from which to get logs for raft" (Rose, Jr. 1959). The men had found the river too hazardous to cross with heavy wagons, and decided to build a log raft and make a ferry to transport women, children and wagons, an enterprise that would take three or four days. To them the trees were free timber.

This was an ingenious idea, except that cottonwood trees, according to the Mojaves' age-old way of thinking, were *their* trees, and trespassers had no right to cut them down. To the Mojaves, cottonwoods in their desert oasis should be cut sparingly to make poles for their *abahs* (houses). Moreover, the soft inside bark of the cottonwoods was the material from which Mojave women painstakingly made their clothing. Unwittingly, the emigrants were stealing Mojave lumber, Mojave dry-goods, and Mojave shade from the blazing summer suns. Their hundreds of animals were trampling over the places along the river, where, after summer overflow, Mojave farmers planted their crops.

The Rose party was too thoroughly shaken by the attack to attempt to cross the river and go on to California. San Bernardino was only 200 miles distant and Albuquerque was 560 miles. Nevertheless, they were determined to return to Albuquerque. Thus, this group reascended the pass, met the other division of the train, and salvaged as much of their provisions as they could haul with seventeen head of cattle, ten horses, and two mules. Not far from the pass they met two west-bound trains, and persuaded the members that it was too dangerous to continue west.

Their plight was described by Colonel Bonneville, commanding the Department of New Mexico, in a report to the General of the Army, dated November 7, 1858:

> A large party of emigrants, who had taken Beale's route to California, were totally defeated, with the loss of all their stock, provisions, etc., by the Mohave Indians, at the crossing of the Colorado River, and must have starved had they not fortunately, on their return, met another party traveling about eight miles behind them. In a short time all were reduced to the most destitute and deplorable condition, having nothing to eat but the few work-oxen left, and hundreds of miles away from the settlements or assistance. They succeeded in inform-ing Major Backus, then in command of the Albuquerque, of their situation, and he sent out a supply of commissary stores sufficient to bring them into settlement. In consideration of their perfect haplessness—being amongst a people not able to appreciate their condition, and speaking a different language—I found it indispensably necessary to give them additional

assistance, there being a large number of women and children left perfectly destitute (1859:258).

In this flight at the river, the emigrants lost practically all of their possessions. Eleven men were wounded and one man was killed. Mojave casualties were not definitely known. Seventeen were killed within sight of the emigrants' camp (Rose, Jr. 1959:26); others were said to have been wounded or killed. The disappearance of Mr. and Mrs. Bentner, their son and one daughter was interpreted as a massacre. Subsequent investigation showed that this wagon was followed from the mountains by Hualapais and attacked by them. There were, however, seven renegade Mojaves in the attacking party, all of whom were killed.

CHAPTER VIII:
BITTERNESS ROAD

The events culminating in the establishment of Fort Mojave, and in the United States military control of the Mojaves, have been told so erroneously since 1859 that the actual facts are hard to believe. When rumors and hearsay are disregarded, and the official reports of the War Department are used as the source of information, a different story of the establishment of Fort Mojave and the military subjugation of the Mojaves emerges.

The army crackdown on the Mojave Indians was touched off by General N. S. Clarke, commander of the Military Department of California with headquarters in distant San Francisco, who became very concerned when word reached him of the attack on the emigrant train. Believing that the reported hostilities of the Mojaves signalled the beginning of a general Indian uprising incited by the Mormons, and that the situation was too dangerous to delay action until he could hear from Washington, General Clarke decided to spike further trouble by posting troops in a position to cover Beale's Crossing and control the Indians along the route. He ordered Lieutenant Colonel William Hoffman, of the 6th Infantry, to cover the crossing at the Mojave Villages and, in order to further expedite matters, he sent the colonel in advance of his troops to locate a post site that would be within striking distance of the Indians. Colonel Hoffman with his escort had already penetrated into the Mojave Desert, becoming more and more convinced that the country was impassable for troop movements and impossible for a military post, when General Clarke received orders from the Secretary of War to post two companies, provisioned for six months, with as little delay as possible "at the point upon the right bank of the Colorado, where the wagon road passed over by E. F. Beale, Esq., in 1857 crosses the river" (Cooper

1858). A map was enclosed showing the route to be followed, and the exact location of the post.

The War Department had long-range reasons for ordering a post at this particular location on Beale's route. The road from Fort Smith to the Colorado was planned for a military road with posts located at strategic intervals to guarantee year-round military mobility and wide-range striking power. The Mojaves were only one factor in a complicated set of circumstances in the protection of the West, but unfortunately for them, a strategic point for military protection lay at the Colorado River crossing in the heart of their Mojave Valley. It was also unfortunate for the Mojaves that the Army officers in charge of establishing this post were strangers who assumed them to be enemies, and treated them accordingly.

Before General Clarke was able to reach Colonel Hoffman with these explicit orders from the Secretary of War, Colonel Hoffman's reconnaissance party had an encounter with the Mojaves that caused the General to launch a full-scale punitive campaign against them. This incident was the calamity in Mojave history that marked the end of the Mojave nation as a free people and placed them under the military custody of the United States.

Beaver Lake was in the southern end of the territory of the *Matha lyathum*, or north Mojaves, whose chief was *Homoseh quahote* (spelled *Sikahot* by Ives). *Homoseh quahote* was also the Great Chieftain of the Mojaves. In view of the long-standing misconceptions of what actually happened, Colonel Hoffman's own account of the incident at Beaver Lake is quoted from his official report to General Clarke, dated January 16, 1859.

> I deem it proper to report, for the information of the general commanding the department, an affair between my escort, under the command of Lieutenant A. B. Chapman, first dragoons, and the Mojave Indians, which occurred at Beaver lake, on the morning of the 9th instant.
>
> Beaver Lake lies between the bluffs of the Colorado and the river, and was, doubtless, once a part of the channel, forming one of its deep bends; but the river, cutting through the narrow neck of land which separated the head and foot of the bend, and closing at the outlet, a horseshoe shaped lake (now dry) was formed of bright green water, quite unlike that of a river.
>
> The crest of the bluffs which border the Colorado is nine miles from the river, and we had scarcely crossed it before

we saw several smokes appearing in succession down the river, at intervals of a few miles. With the glass, I could see no person; nor did we see any other sign of the presence of Indians until our camp, which was located near the lake, was established. Then some five or six were seen running from a thicket which was on our right toward the camp, and they came as if they were sure of a welcome. They proved to be Pai-Utes, and soon a dozen or more were making themselves quite at home. Among them was one who was represented to be the chief. They said their camp was not far below, and that the Mojaves were further down; and that their chief, with many of their people, would be up to see me in the morning.

In a little while a number of Mohaves came into camp, all young men of fine athletic appearance, armed with new bows, and an unusual number of arrows. All told the same story about the coming of the chiefs with their people. They behaved very well; but there was an independence in their manners that could not fail to attract attention.

Some of them brought in grass for our horses, which was paid for in tobacco and empty barley sacks. At sunset, they were told to leave the camp, and cautioned not to come near it at night, or the sentinels would shoot them.[1]

Being anxious to examine the valley above and below this point, I determined to move at the usual hour the following morning, and proceeded down the river a day's march, expecting to meet and have a talk with the Mohaves by the way.

Accordingly, we marched before seven o'clock, and had gone but about a mile when we saw in front of us, at different points, parties of twenty or thirty Mohaves, who kept aloof from us, while some Pai-Utes, the same we had seen the night before, came to us and asked some questions about our destination. All of these Indians, as on the previous evening, were well armed with bows and arrows, the Mohaves being painted and entirely naked, except a piece of cotton cloth suspended from the waist. The morning was exceedingly cold, as the night before had been, and nothing but something extraordinary could have induced them to expose themselves to severe weather. As we proceeded, some half dozen, one or two of whom could speak Spanish, approached us and asked some

---

[1]This inhospitable behavior would have been offensive to the Mojaves (Stillman 1989).

questions; but they were evidently much excited, and seemed to doubt whether they were safe or not.

In about three miles the broken character of the bench above the river bottom, over which we were marching, became so broken that we were compelled to leave it and take to the bottom. Very soon this became very uneven and so covered with a thick undergrowth that we could only advance by cutting our way through, with much time and labor.

Before undertaking this, I halted the command and went forward to see how far this obstruction continued, and finding that there was much of it, and that, besides, gullies were washed from the bluffs to the river, difficult of crossing, I decided to advance no further.

I could not but notice, that in passing through this place, after opening the way, I would have steep bluffs on one hand and a dense thicket on the other; a situation that would place me entirely at the mercy of an enemy, and by placing myself in so hazardous a position, an attack might be invited which otherwise would not have been ventured on. After retracing my steps to the vicinity of our camp, I decided to examine the valley above, but a mile or two brought us to a halt, owing to the broken character of the country and its being cut close to the bluffs by a bend of the river. I therefore returned to the lake camp, selecting, this time, the most defensible position I could find; the lake being in rear, and a bluff bank, about the height of a man's breast, in front; the left was a narrow point between the bank and lake, and on the right, the weak point, was a close thicket. After establishing the camp, I examined the trail leading to the crossing of the river, and returning in an hour or two, some Mojaves made their appearance in camp soon after. They were armed and independent as before, and even arrogant. Some of them begged for tobacco, but none would bring grass for it. One, who spoke Spanish, said one chief would be in to see me that evening, and two others, with all their people, including women and children, would arrive in the morning. Very soon he left, saying he would meet the chief and come with him.

I told him to tell the chief our camp was small, and he must not bring many with him—twelve or fifteen; the others might remain just below the camp and make a fire to warm themselves by. The chief did not come, and the others were sent out of camp at sunset, with the same cautions as on the previous evening. There was evidently no good feeling toward us on the part of the Indians, and I had no confidence in what they told me of the coming of the chiefs on a friendly visit. I looked upon this as a mere pretext to gain time for the assembling of warriors. To be prepared for any emergency, Lieutenant Chapman made the most judicious arrangements for the defense of the camp against a night attack, and every man, being fully armed, was assigned a particular place. Soon after dark six Indians were seen to leave the thicket, passing to our front, but on hearing the sentinel call for the guard they ran back. About ten o'clock, fifteen or twenty approached a sentinel; who fired at them, when they immediately ran back yelling to their cover. This showed that there was a watchful enemy about us, and every man of the command remained at his post all night, which was very cold and inclement. At four o'clock in the morning reveille was sounded and preparations were commenced to march at the usual time. The hostile attitude taken by the Indians left little room to doubt that we could not remain another twenty-four hours in the valley without a collision with the Mohave nation. Everything remained quiet until about sunrise on the 9th, when our preparations for the march were nearly completed. A few Pai-Utes, known by their dress, showed themselves near the camp, on the edge of the thicket, one hundred and fifty to two hundred yards distant; and soon Mohaves began to collect rapidly.

About the same time an arrow was found near where the Indian was who was shot at by the sentinel; another was found in the brush which concealed the sentinel; and two others were found in the camp, one of them sticking in a tree. These were tokens of hostile feelings not to be misunderstood. As our preparations progressed the Indians were rapidly increasing in force, making fires in the grass closer and closer to camp; their numbers being evidently considerably greater than ours. These hostile demonstrations, and the insult of shooting arrows into our camp, determined me to attack them as soon as the packing of the mules was completed. When all was ready, I ordered the pack and wagon, with a guard of six men, to move on in the direction of our return march, and when they were out of the way, I directed Lieutenant Chapman, with one platoon of his command dismounted, which covered all the ground from which the enemy could be seen, to fire on them. This was done in so spirited a manner, and effectually, that a very few rounds sufficed to drive the whole body of the enemy into the thicket.

A number were seen to fall, killed and wounded, perhaps ten or twelve in all.

Having accomplished all that I purposed, and all that could be expected of the small force under Lieutenant Chapman, I ordered the escort to be put in march to follow the train. Soon after, a large number of Mohaves, 250 to 300, made a faint show of following us, but a few well-directed shots on some scattering ones, who came within long carbine range, quickly induced them to retire.

While we were preparing to march, Indians were calling out to us in a taunting tone; and one of them imitated the words of command as they were given; another, being not far from where the arrow was found, imitated the actions of those he had seen a few moments before examining the tracks.[2] If I had allowed this insolence to pass unnoticed they would have hooted us out of the valley with shouts of derision. They were probably led to expect that we would attempt to cross the Colorado, from the reconnaissance I had made of the intermediate ground the evening before; and they knew that while passing through the thicket which lined the trail they would have us completely in their power; hence, possibly, their inactivity while we were packing. Their numbers had been increasing from the hour of our arrival, and none showed themselves who were not prepared for battle.

It gives me pleasure to add that the vigilance, energy, and soldierly bearing of Lieutenant Chapman, on the night previous to, and on the morning of, the affair entitled him to high commendation; and his men deserve great praise for their readiness to meet an enemy of greatly superior numbers.

The route over which I have passed to the Colorado I have no hesitation in saying is wholly impassable for trains, or for a larger body of troops than my escort; and any expedition against the Mohaves must be made by the river, if it be navigable, from Fort Yuma. A command should be sent of sufficient size, I would very respectfully suggest, to operate on

---

[2]The Mojaves were "playing" with the United States forces in a traditional method for testing out the attitude of visitors (Stillman 1990).

both sides of the river at once; their supplies for a few days being carried on pack mules or camels, and a steamboat accompanying them to serve as a depot (Hoffman 1860a).

There are definitely two sides to this story. Colonel Hoffman with his small party of soldiers, surrounded in wild country by a large number of Indians whose language and customs they did not understand and whose intentions they believed to be hostile, had ample basis for apprehension. On the other hand, the Indians had justifiable reason for investigating the purposes of a party of soldiers who were reconnoitering in their land. Whether the Mojaves actually intended to attack Hoffman's party when the troops entered the Beaver Lake region cannot be proved or disproved on the basis of the facts recorded. Colonel Hoffman obviously thought that they did hold such intentions, as his statements and precautions show.

To Hoffman, the smoke signals portended danger, the ordinary all-weather garb of breechcloth and paint boded something extraordinary, the scouts who came to ascertain the purposes of strangers and to announce the coming of their chiefs were decoys, the visit of the chiefs was a hoax. On the other hand, the Mojaves had reason to feel that the soldiers were hostile. Hoffman's warning to the scouts to stay away from his camp after nightfall or they would be shot, and his message that only twelve to fifteen Indians might visit him were rebuffs. Breaking camp in the face of a proclaimed visit by the chieftain was an insult. To the Mojaves, these were signs of hostility as unmistakable as the sentry's shot.

There is no doubt that the Mojaves became hostile; that they mocked the troops, shot four souvenir arrows into the bushes around the camp, started to burn the grass; or that the warriors began to collect. There is positive evidence that Hoffman's sentry fired the first shot, that it was the troops who opened fire on the mocking Indians, and that ten or twelve Mojaves were seen to fall, killed or wounded.

Regardless of later differences of opinion regarding offensive and defensive actions in the Beaver Lake incident, the commanding general at the time based his immediate military operations against the Mojaves on the premise that they attacked Colonel Hoffman's escort, and needed a lesson that would teach them to respect and fear the might and striking power of the United States Army.

Taking at face value Hoffman's report that troops could not be moved through the Mojave Desert to Beale's Crossing, General Clarke decided to move by the Colorado River, and to throw enough troops against the Mojaves to either cow or beat them into submission.

General Clarke forwarded Colonel Hoffman's report to the War Department with a message that he would leave his San Francisco Headquarters immediately, ". . . to institute operations against those Indians, and . . . also, to inflict chastisement . . ." He also ordered Hoffman to command the Colorado River expedition, to establish a post at Beale's Crossing and ". . . march against the Mohaves and Pai-Utes who lately opposed your reconnaissance," stating that his change in plans was due to "opposition made to your late reconnaissance, and the attack on your escort by the Mohaves, together with your representation of the difficulty of crossing any considerable force over the desert at or near the 35th parallel." The heart of his order read: "These tribes, and all others who assume a hostile attitude, must be brought to submission. Do not temporize. If a blow must be struck, let it be effective." He ordered further that:

> If subdued by the appearance of your force, the Mohaves and Pai-Utes decline the combat, then, through friendly Indians, communicate with them, demand the surrender of the chiefs who made the attack on your party, and hostages for their further conduct, or tell them that you will lay waste their fields; and that the troops to be stationed on the river will not permit them hereafter to cultivate their lands in peace (Clarke 1858).

Hoffman followed General Clarke's orders to the letter. At Fort Yuma he mobilized his incoming troops, organized his base of supplies and his supply line, and sent couriers among the Quechans to notify them of his objective of establishing a military post among the Mojaves. He assured the excited Quechans that the Indians had a choice between peace and war, and that no peaceful Indian would be harmed. If any of the Quechan sympathizers had been inclined to aid their old allies, they subsided when they saw the soldiers pouring into Fort Yuma. Not a bow was raised nor the slightest movement made to harass or impede the troops. Hoffman's spectacular demonstration of military strength moved up toward the Mojaves on both sides of the river, with the steamers *Colorado* and *General Jessup* standing by, while a command of dragoons marched across the Mojave Desert to meet him at the Colorado. When this movement, with its frightening show of soldiery, converged at Beale's Crossing, Hoffman established the post without resistance or bloodshed. The Mojaves had no choice but surrender.

In a report to General Clarke, dated April 24, 1859 at the new post "Camp Colorado," later renamed "Fort Mojave," Hoffman stated the terms of surrender imposed upon the tribe:

> 1st. They must offer no opposition to the establishment of posts and roads in and through their country, when and where the government chooses; and the property and lives of whites travelling through their country must be secured.
>
> 2nd. As security for their future good conduct they must place in my hands one hostage from each of the six bands.
>
> 3rd. They must place in my hands the chief who commanded at the threatened attack on my camp in January last.
>
> 4th. They must place in my hands three of those who were engaged in the attack on the emigrant party at this spot last summer.
>
> The first, second, and third conditions were complied with without hesitation. Indeed, the first [second?] one not being properly interpreted, all chiefs but one stepped forward to give themselves up. On its being properly explained, one only remained as hostage, and he proved to be the chief, "Cairrook", who was to be given up under the third condition, and I accepted him in this double capacity. In relation to the fourth condition they stated that the emigrant party was followed from the mountains by the Walupies, who made the attack upon them; that there were only seven Mohaves present, who were killed, and that they are now at war with those people on account of difficulties which grew out of that affair. Their statement in relation to the attack by the Walupies is corroborated by the accounts given of the affair by the emigrants themselves. I then required that they should give up to me three men for the part taken by the Mohaves in the massacre, to be dealt with as I might see proper. This was complied with, and to-day I have told the chiefs that these men would go to Fort Yuma, to be sent back at the general's pleasure.
>
> Of the nine men in my possession one is a chief, two are the sons of chiefs, four are the brothers, and two are the nephews of the chiefs. Besides this strong proof of the sincerity of their submission, all have expressed, in the strongest of terms, their anxiety to be at peace with whites, and their gratification at having a post in their country . . . . As far as I

could learn there is nothing remaining among these Indians of the property taken from the party of emigrants last summer, and no restitution could be made (Hoffman 1860b).

Hoffman's peace terms contained the agreement that the Mojaves were to allow government posts and roads anywhere in their country, and safe passage to white people traveling through their territory. Although "posts and roads" imply the taking of land which they occupy, the terms conveyed no hint of lands to be taken by or for white settlers; the whites were specifically mentioned as "traveling through."

In item three of his terms, Hoffman *did not accuse* the Mojaves of an attack on his escort at Beaver Lake. He asked for the chief "who commanded at the threatened attack." This statement is more compatible with his original report of the incident than with General Clarke's interpretation of it as an attack.

The report exonerates the Mojaves from the attack on the emigrant train, and places the blame squarely on the Hualapai and seven renegade Mojaves who helped them. Nevertheless, disrepute and wholesale punishment was brought upon the entire Mojave nation. The actual details of Hoffman's humiliating subjugation of the Mojaves is contained in the follow-up report, requested by General Clarke. Hoffman's description of the happenings follows:

> After the interviews had with some of the chiefs, as heretofore reported, finding that their people had been trading beans to soldiers and citizens, in order to discourage the friendly feeling this traffic countenanced, I prohibited all persons from having any communications whatever with any Indians in the Mohave valley. The consequence was, as I desired, that none came near us from that time.
>
> On the morning after my arrival at the crossing, I sent word to the Mohave chiefs that if they desired peace I would receive the submission of themselves and their people on the second morning thereafter at ten o'clock. All must come in punctually at that hour or they would not be received at all. I did not require that they should bring their families with them.
>
> In the meantime, on the afternoon of my arrival and the next day, I made a reconnaissance of the ground on this side of the river opposite our camp, and constructed in the camp a place in which to hold the council, should the Indians come in; a matter which I looked upon as exceedingly doubtful. In the event of their not coming, my plans for immediate hostilities

were arranged to commence as soon as the appointed hour had expired.

Believing that these Indians deserved a severe chastisement for their many offenses, and believing also that any settlement with them would be more lasting if it could be preceded by a defeat, I was not willing to encourage them to submit without a trial of their ability to resist us; and I therefore gave them no intimation of the conditions I would impose upon them, but let them clearly understand that they must come in prepared to assent to any demand I might make of them.

If they capitulated on these terms it would be conclusive proof that they felt that they were wholly at my mercy, and would give every assurance that their fear of punishment, which alone controls Indians, would prevent their ever again placing themselves in a similar jeopardy.

On the evening of the 22nd, I announced to the officers of the command that if the Mohaves came in to sue for peace, I had determined that, under no circumstances, would I permit them to leave the camp until a satisfactory settlement had been made. To this end I made arrangements to meet any emergency.

On the morning of the 23rd, before the hour appointed arrived, it was announced that the Mohaves were coming, and some four or five hundred men, preceded by their chiefs, were entering camp. I had directed Captain Burton to receive them, and to inform me when they were all seated.

They evidently came in under very great apprehension; and the preparations which had been made to receive them, which they could not fail to detect, were not calculated to allay their fears. Under this influence a number of them turned back, but the chiefs went after them and brought many in. Some two hundred and fifty to three hundred assembled in and about the council-house, and a hundred and fifty to two hundred remained outside the camp.

When all was prepared, I opened the council by reminding them that I had allowed them to choose between peace and war. If they desired peace, they might come in and submit to my terms.

They had preferred peace, and were then there, not to talk, but to listen to what I had to say. At this point they manifested a good deal of alarm, and the two interpreters, Pasqual and Jose Maria, becoming alarmed also, I had much difficulty in restoring quiet. When the excitement subsided, I had the conditions which I had imposed on them carefully explained to them; and, as I have already reported, they were all, without hesitation, complied with.

After all was amicably arranged, a marked sensation of relief and gladness was plainly depicted on the countenances of the crowd of Indians; and, on my telling the chief that I would now listen to anything they might desire to say, each of them expressed the happiness it afforded them that I had permitted them to have peace, and their gratification that a post was to be established in their country. They said the country was mine, and I might do what I pleased with it: all they asked was that they might be permitted to live in it, &c. The following day these assurances were repeated to me in stronger terms; and, since it was palpable before them that in case of war at any future date they must be driven from the valley, I think it may be confidently relied on that they will never again, as a body, give occasion for sending troops against them. Their whole demeanor, from the time I entered their country until I left it, was that of a subdued people asking for mercy.

They never before had seen any but small parties of white people, and the presence of so large a number of troops filled them with surprise and fear; an effect produced also on other river tribes, the consequence of which will be to prevent, at any future day, all thoughts of combined hostilities (Hoffman 1860c).[3]

---

[3]Hal Davidson wrote of this episode:

"I was about 15 years old when the first Federal soldiers were placed in the valley to keep peace among the Indians or Mohaves. I made many trips to the Fort Mohave pass as the soldiers were very kind people and gave us food. And I also witnessed the treaty of peace between the Federal government troops and the Mohave Indians. The soldiers' campus was made of sticks and brush but [they were] well armed for their protection and at this place the conference took place.

"I do not know the big white Chief [Hoffman] who represented the California government but I know our representative—Chief Hamuse-qu-hote. Means Orator of Stars.

"Chief Hamuse-qu-hote is over 6 feet tall and not heavy built but the scars on his breast show that he has fought many people for justice or to carry out the set up of our government. His hair is long, he's painted in red, white and black, and armed and [wears] few feathers on his head. He stood with the white Chief, both hands clasped as they stood face to face. When our Chief spoke he left work on No. 8. He said it is going to be very difficult as we have different languages, and [as] to making

(continued...)

On April 26, Hoffman broke up his Colorado River expedition, well satisfied that two companies of infantry and a detachment of artillery could control the thoroughly subdued Mojaves. He left Brevet Major Lewis A. Armistead in command of the temporary post, Camp Colorado, pending further orders.

General Clarke and Colonel Hoffman both doubted that the Secretary of War would maintain a permanent military post at this location after he had reviewed all the facts submitted in their reports; and for good reason. Transportation of troops and supplies by land was impracticable if not impossible; transportation by water via Fort Yuma was slow and costly; natural resources for subsisting troops were non-existent; the intemperate climate was debilitating and unhealthful for troops; and finally, the awful character of the desert, when it was actually known to emigrants, would discourage the use of Beale's road to California. The answer of the Secretary of War to Clarke's discouraging recommendations, dated April 30, did not arrive until June. Regardless of adverse conditions, the post was to be maintained as previously ordered (Cooper 1860).

Major Armistead, five days after he was left in command at Beale's Crossing, voiced his opinion directly to the Adjutant-General in the War Department. He thought the post was advantageously located, with plenty of good water, wood and grass, that supplies could be sent up the river without any trouble, or hauled from San Bernardino over passable roads; and that the Indians were unlikely to cause trouble, but if hostile could be readily suppressed by destroying their crops and starving them. He announced that he had changed the name of the post from Camp Colorado to Fort Mojave, and contradicted his commander's recommendation relative to its permanency: "I am of the opinion that the great mineral wealth of this country will lead to its early settlement; in which event, the necessity of a military post is obvious" (Armistead 1860a). This last statement proved later to be true, but before the

---

3(...continued)
friends we are to suffer a great loss. On properties and ourselves.
    "We will not hear your mission to our country.
    "The White Chief spoke that they have come to make friends. That there is plenty room for education and that the government they represent is the white government and if the Mohave Indians prove to be good citizens, that the white government will protect their properties and will always be brothers and sisters. That they will suffer together any losses and gain together what human life requires. Freedom and liberty for all. The Mohave Indians acknowledged the White people ways and assisted them every possible way to this date . . ." (Davidson 1935).

summer was over the Major had reason to reverse most of his other snap judgments.

Fort Mojave was located at "Beale's Crossing" at the Mojave Villages on the east side of the Colorado River, on the edge of a gravel plateau seventy-five feet above the river. Major Armistead put the soldiers to work making crude barracks, a guard house, hospital and stockade, Indian fashion, from willow poles and brush. Since they had no wagons, all the materials had to be packed on their backs, sometimes a mile or more. Then the thermometer started climbing to 120 and 130 degrees, and the river began its age-old rampage, spilling the flood waters over the trails and slipping into mosquito-breeding sloughs. The supply steamer bringing rations and clothing from Fort Yuma got stuck on a sand bar in the low waters of May, and could not navigate the heavy currents and swollen waters of June flood time. The overflow mired the trails and bogged the passage of pack trains from San Bernardino. By late June, the soldiers were ragged, barefooted, and almost starved, and either sick or half sick.

The Mojaves, too, were on short rations, waiting for the ground to dry for September planting. They had gone peaceably about their business, with no show of hostility or rancor against the occupation forces. Then, on June 30, came trouble. A Quechan courier brought word to Armistead that the hostages sent to Fort Yuma had attempted to escape. Four had succeeded, five were killed, among them Cairook.[4]

The Mojaves, who had been abiding by the terms of the peace treaty, were appalled and alarmed by the tragedy of their leader. The attempted escape is one of the saddest stories in Mojave history. Ives tells it well. He was in Washington at the time of the occurrence, writing his report on the recent Colorado River survey. He had described the great kindness shown by Cairook to him and Lieutenant Tipton during their stay in the Mojave Valley. His journal entry of March 23, 1858, telling of their departure from the valley, reads:

> Cairook came to bid us farewell. I was never before so struck with his noble appearance. When he shook hands his head was almost level with mine as he stood beside the mule on

---

[4]According to Mojave oral history, as reported in 1903 to A. L. Kroeber by *Chooksa homar* (Jo Nelson), who had been a youngster in the late 1850s, only two of the hostages were killed. Seven escaped by jumping into the river and swimming downstream, overpowering soldiers who had left their guns behind when they grabbed a boat to pursue the fleeing Mojaves. Three reached the Arizona shore and hid, eventually reaching Parker before the other four. That they had survived was apparently not known at Fort Mojave (Kroeber and Kroeber 1973:vii, 25-26).

which I was riding. He indicated his wishes that we might
have a successful trip, and remained watching the train until it
was out of sight, waving his hand and smiling his adieus. We
all felt regret at parting with him, for he had proved himself a
staunch friend (Ives 1861).

A footnote to this entry reads:

This excellent chief is no longer living. Not many
months after our departure a difficulty occurred between the
Mojaves and a party of emigrants, in which some of the latter
were killed. A detachment of troops, subsequently ordered to
the valley, was fired upon by the Indians, and a large force was
sent to obtain satisfaction. The Mojaves made peace by
surrendering eight or nine of their principal men as security for
the future good behavior of the rest. Cairook volunteered to go
as hostage, and was confined, with his companions, in the
guard-house.[5] The restraint soon became irksome and galling
to their wild natures, and to Cairook in particular it was almost
intolerable. His faithful follower, Ireteba, visited him several
times during his confinement, and one day made an eloquent
appeal in his behalf to Lieutenant Tipton, who was again on
duty at the fort. He recounted in moving terms the services
Cairook had rendered, both to Lieutenant Whipple's party and
to my own, and begged that he might be set free. Of course
Lieutenant Tipton had no power to grant the request, but this
Ireteba could not comprehend, and went away grievously
disappointed, saying that if the "commandante" (a title he had
formerly applied to me) were here he knew the favor would not
be refused.

When the chief learned the failure of the mission he
made a characteristic proposition to his brother captives for the
termination of his own and their confinement. At certain hours
they were all permitted to come out for fresh air upon the porch
of the guard-house, and he agreed, being a very powerful man,
to seize and hold the sentinel and allow the rest to escape. The

---

[5]He wanted to take the headman down to Yuma to the jail. "Hell hole." That's what they were
called. They were called the jail. But then our people loved their head man and said, "I'm a
nephew. Take me instead. Don't take him." Another nephew said, "I'm another nephew, take me."
And the third one said the same. The rest . . . the others said, "Take me. Take me." And he had
nine volunteers and he said, "That's enough. I said ten, but that will be enough" (Stillman 1988).

heroic and generous project was executed. The following
morning as the Indians were taking an airing in front of the
guard-house, they made a sudden rush down the hill towards
the river, Cairook at the same instant pinioning the sentinel in
his arms. He was bayoneted on the spot by members of the
guard. The fugitives were fired upon. Some were killed and
some escaped. None were retaken alive.[6] The survivors
carried to the tribe the story of their chief's self-sacrifice, and
the only son of Cairook, a fine boy, has since been regarded by
the Mojaves almost with veneration (Ives 1861).

Armistead sent word to the Mojaves that the escaped hostages
must be turned over to him at once. Then he dispatched, on July 3, a
communique to General Clarke reporting the Yuma jail break and asking
for instructions, for at that time the common military practice was to
punish the tribe for offenses of any of its members. He wrote:

> I have the honor to report that information was brought
> me by a Yuma Indian living now in this vicinity, on the 30th
> ultimo, that the Mohave prisoners had escaped from the guard
> at Fort Yuma. The same Indian brought word that the Mohaves
> did not want to fight. I sent word to them by him, that if they
> wished to be friends, they must give up the four prisoners that
> had escaped.
>
> The Mohaves have behaved well, so far; they have
> committed no hostile act, and appear quite alarmed; they are
> evidently not a warlike people. They are coming in and out of
> camp as usual, but only in small numbers. What does the
> general wish me to do?
>
> If I have to fight, I have men enough, if the two
> companies of infantry here are kept up to the organization. . .
> If the General wishes me to attack these Indians, the best plan,

---

[6] "One of the men, the old one of the bunch of the three young men—Cairook was his
name—said to the young men, 'You're all young. I'm years ahead of you. I've had a lot of years
already that I've spent of my life. When it's lunch time, all the guards go to their lunch except for
that one up there. I'll go up and hold him while you men dive into the water.'

  The river is swollen then. So guess what happened? Of course the guard shot him right
away. Maybe stabbed him, anyway, killed the old man 'cause he said, 'He was old anyway and the
others were young.' So they escaped. They dove and swam under water until they reached the
banks, which were covered with willows and cottonwoods, and hid 'til night time. In the dark they
moved staying hidden" (Stillman 1988).

if I may be permitted to say so, would be to have a light-draft boat. . . . With such a boat troops could be landed at any point on the river throughout the year, and the Indians' crops destroyed, if nothing more, which would result in death from starvation, of many (Armistead 1860b).

General Clarke referred this ticklish problem to the General-in-Chief, who referred it to the Secretary of War. It was not until August 20 that the Secretary returned the report to the General-in-Chief, with the comment:

The escape of the hostages was what was to be expected if an opportunity offered. Of itself, it will not be made the ground for hostilities against the Mohaves. The plan of taking Indian hostages for indefinite periods is attended with no useful results, but rather the contrary, and will be prohibited.

In the meantime, Major Armistead received an unexpected answer to his question about punishment for the hostage affair. A series of offenses culminated in a tribal explosion.

According to Major Armistead's report to General Clarke, the Mojaves on the night of July 20 stampeded sixteen head of mules belonging to a California-bound mail party that had camped two or three miles from the fort, and on the following evening they drove the mail party itself into the fort. On the 22nd some Indians were seen near a dead mule, which presumably they had killed. Armistead ordered a party of soldiers to fire into this group from ambush. On the night (the 22nd) from 250 to 300 Mojaves collected at the spot from which they had driven the mail party. Armistead wanted to bring on an action, but the Mojaves would not be provoked to an engagement. Several days later (the 31st) a small party of Indians shot at the post patrol.

Major Armistead's report did not say why the Mojaves stole the mules and attacked the mail party, why a Mojave crowd gathered at the place where the mail carrier had camped, and a small band of Mojaves shot at the post patrol. Nor did it mention any attempt on his part to investigate the reasons for the Mojaves's show of bad feeling, nor to have the offenders brought in for punishment. Instead he decided to punish the tribe. He reported to General Clarke:

I have the honor to report that I left this post on the night of the 4th instant, with twenty-five picked men of F company, sixth infantry, my object being to surprise the Indians by keeping around on the Mesa, and in that way get below them. Lieutenant Marshall left next morning with the same number of picked men in the same direction. By morning, I found myself near one of the largest ranches on the river, (Ireteba's), about twelve miles below the post; by crawling up, got a shot at three "bucks" planting beans; killed one. The firing soon raised the whole valley. I selected good grounds across a small slough. The Indians came up very bravely all around us, but they were met with coolness and confidence on the part of our men. The firing had lasted some thirty minutes, when Lieutenant Marshall, hearing it, came up; the Indians retreated. After some twenty minutes, they came up again as boldly as before; they were met in the same way. After some fifteen minutes fighting, they retreated again as boldly as before; they were met in the same way. After some fifteen minutes fighting, they retreated again. Some time having elapsed, I thought they had had enough, and commenced my return to the post. We did not go far before they came up again; this time more boldly than ever. The ground was favorable to them, being full of little sand hillocks. They stood our firing very well, coming up to within twenty or thirty paces; but in about thirty minutes, they had to run. This time, they were apparently so well satisfied as to omit their whoop of defiance, which had accompanied their other retreats. I do not know how many Indians there were; there was a great many.

Each time the Indians retreated, we went over the ground they had occupied; and, in that way, know how many they left dead on the field. Twenty-three were counted. Our loss was three men (of I company) slightly wounded (Armistead 1860b).

Major Armistead's report of this battle does not altogether tally with the Mojaves' story. Both sides say that the fighting lasted most of the day, and that a great many Mojaves took part. Major Armistead reported twenty-three Indians killed, three United States soldiers slightly wounded. The Mojaves say that in the battle, which in their Tribal Records is classed as "the first and last battle with the Federal Troops," Mojave men, women, and children were slaughtered by the hundreds, and that remnants of bones and hair were scattered all over the battle ground. No one knows for certain what the casualties were, but apparently more Mojaves were killed than Major Armistead reported. His men, cool headed and crack shots, averaged less than "ten rounds per man," or somewhat under 500 rounds. Twenty-three dead Indians seems a small casualty list under the circumstances.

The Mojaves' version of the wrongs that led up to the fight says that the mail party tore up a melon patch, and when the Indians asked them to pay for the damage the men and the soldiers only laughed. The cold-blooded sneak killing of a Mojave farmer on Ireteba's ranch was the last straw. The Mojaves went berserk. Underneath the surface was a fear that the invaders would destroy their crops and starve the people. These Mojaves still believed that they were entitled to plant along the river that *Mastamho* had given their fathers long ago. They fought, and lost. They knew, now, that many warriors with arrows were helpless against a few soldiers with guns.

The chieftains sued for peace. On August 31, Major Armistead reported to General Clarke that he had made peace. "All the terms that I could demand of them were that they should behave themselves, and give up the bend in the river where the mules were herded, and never come on it."

Major Armistead learned that these peacefully inclined Mojaves were unleashed fury when pushed too far, and that the tactics of destroying crops might be costly. "I am of the opinion," he wrote General Clarke, "that it would not be prudent with a small command to destroy their fields" (Armistead 1860c).

The older Mojaves around Needles in 1905 remembered "Armistead," and the younger ones had heard about him and hated the name. The man behind the expedition, General Clarke, was unknown to them. The Secretary of War commended General Clarke and his men for the expedition against the Mojaves, "which had terminated successfully."

REFERENCES CITED

Armistead, Major Lewis A.

    1860a   Letter to Adjutant General, Department of War, May 1, 1859. Report of the Secretary of War, 1859. U.S. 36th Congress, 1st Session. HR Executive Document, Vol. II:405-406. Washington, D.C.: George W. Bowman, Printer.

    1860b   Letter to Brig. Gen. Newman S. Clarke, Commander of the Military Department of California, July 3, 1859. Report of the Secretary of War, 1859. U.S. 36th Congress, 1st Session. HR Executive Document, Vol. II:414-415. Washington, D.C.: George W. Bowman, Printer.

    1860c   Letter to Brig. Gen. Newman S. Clarke, Commander of the Military Department of California, August 31, 1859. Report of the Secretary of War, 1859. U.S. 36th Congress, 1st Session. HR Executive Document, Vol. II:421. Washington, D.C.: George W. Bowman, Printer.

Bancroft, Hubert H.

    1886   The History of California. The Works of Hubert Howe Bancroft I:363-4. San Francisco: The History Company.

    1889   The History of Arizona and New Mexico, 1530-1888. San Francisco: The History Company. (Reprinted: Horn and Wallace, Albuquerque, 1962.)

Beale, Edward F.
1858   Wagon Road from Fort Defiance to the Colorado. HR
            Exec. Doc. No. 124. 35th Cong., 1st Sess. Washington,
            D.C.

1860   Wagon Road--Fort Smith to Colorado River. HR Exec.
            Doc. No. 42:VI. U. S. 36th Congress, 1st session.
            Washington, D.C.

Bolton, Herbert E., transl. and ed.
1925   Spanish Exploration in the Southwest, 1542-1706.
            Original Narratives of Early American History. J.
            Franklin Jameson, gen. ed. New York: Charles Scrib-
            ner's Sons. (Various printings as 1916, 1925. Assigned
            to Barnes & Noble in New York in 1946, reprint 1952.)

1930   Anza's California Expeditions, II. Berkeley: University
            of California Press.

Bonneville, Colonel
1859   Report to the General of the Army, November 7, 1858.
            Report of the Secretary of War 1859. U. S. 36th Con-
            gress, 1st Session, Sen. Exec. Doc. 2. Washington, D.
            C.: Government Printing Office.

Bonsal, Stephen
1912   Edward Fitzgerald Beale; A Pioneer in the Path of
            Empire, 1822-1903. New York and London: G. P.
            Putnam's Sons, Knickerbocker Press.

Brooks, George R., ed.
1977   The Southwest Expedition of Jedediah S. Smith. His
            Personal Account of the Journey to California 1826-
            1827. Glendale, CA: The Arthur C. Clark Company.

Buchanan, James
1858   Message of the President of the United States to the Two
            Houses of Congress at the Commencement of the First
            Session of the Thirty-fifth Congress. U. S. 35th Con-
            gress, 1st Session, Sen. Exec. Doc. 11. Washington,
            D.C. (Also published in *A Compilation of the Messages
            and Papers of the Presidents 1789-1897*, James D.

Richardson, comp., Government Printing Office, Washington, D.C.)

Butler, Elda
1990   Personal Communication to Vane and Bean.

Camp, Charles L.
1923   The Chronicles of George C. Yount, California Pioneer of 1826. California Historical Society Quarterly II (October).

Casebier, Dennis G.
1975   The Mojave Road: Tales of the Mojave Road, No. 5. Norco, CA: Tales of the Mojave Road Publishing Company.

Clarke, Brig. General Newman S., Commander of the Military Department of California
1858   Letter to the General-in-chief of the Army, January 1. *In* Report of the Secretary of War, Vol. II, U. S. 35th Congress, 2nd session, HR Ex. Doc.2. Washington, D. C.: Government Printing Office.

Cleland, Robert Glass
1951   The Cattle on a Thousand Hills: Southern California, 1850-1880. San Marino, CA: Huntington Library.

1952   This Reckless Breed of Men. New York: Knopf.

Cooper, S. Adjutant General, U.S. Army
1858   Orders to Brig. Gen. Newman S. Clarke, Commander of the Military Department of California, Dec. 1. National Archives, Record Group 393, U.S. Department of War, Department of California, Letters Received.

1860   Orders to Brig. Gen. Newman S. Clarke, Commander of the Military Department of California, April 30, 1859. Report of the Secretary of War, 1859. U.S. 36th Congress, 1st Session. HR Executive Document, Vol. II:404-405. Washington, D.C.: George W. Bowman, Printer.

Coues, Elliot
1900   On The Trail of a Spanish Pioneer, The Diary and
               Itinerary of Francisco Garcés (Missionary Priest) in his
               Travels through Sonora, Arizona, And California, 1775-
               1776. New York: Francis P. Harper.

Cullum, Bvt. Maj. Gen. George W.
1891   Biographical Register of the Officers and Graduates of
               the U.S. Military Academy. Vol. I(1-1000), Vol.
               II(1001-2000). 3rd. ed.   Boston: Houghton Mifflin
               Company.

Dale, Harrison C.
1941   The Ashley-Smith Explorations and the Discovery of a
               Central Route to the Pacific, 1822-1829. Revised ed.
               Glendale: Arthur H. Clark.

Davidson, Hal *Oneyuravarya*, Tribal Recorder
1935   History, Mohave Indians Told by Deacon Brown.
               Recorded in "The Big Book", pp. 33-37. (See Sherer
               1966:29 n. 6.)

Floyd, John B., Secretary of War
1858   Orders to Edward F. Beale, December 5, 1857. Depart-
               ment of War, Report of the Secretary of War. U.S. 35th
               Congress, 1st Session, Sen. Exec. Doc. 11, Vol. II:14.
               Washington, D.C.: William A. Harris, Printer.

Forbes, Jack D.
1965   Warriors of the Colorado: The Yumas of the Quechan
               Nation and Their Neighbors. Norman: University of
               Oklahoma Press.

Foreman, Grant
1941   A Pathfinder in the Southwest. Norman, Oklahoma:
               University of Oklahoma Press.

Galvin, John, Translator and Editor
1967   A Record of Travels in Arizona and California, 1775-
               1776, by Francisco Garcés. San Francisco: John Howell-
               Books.

Garland, General John
1858   Letter to Colonel A. S. Johnson, January 24 and 31.
                Report of the Secretary of War, Vol. II:281-82, 287. U.
                S. 35th Congress, 2nd Session, H. Ex. Doc. 2. Washing-
                ton, D. C.: Government Printing Office.

Goetzman, William
1959   Army Exploration in the American West, 1803-1863.
                Yale Publications in American Studies, 4. New Haven,
                CT: Yale University Press.

Hafen, Leroy R., and Ann W. Hafen
1954   Old Spanish Trail. Glendale: Arthur C. Clark.

Hafen, Leroy R., and Carl C. Rister
1950   Western America. 2nd ed. Englewood Cliffs: Prentice
                Hall.

Hayes, Benjamin
n.d.   Emigrant Notes. Manuscript on file at the Bancroft
                Library, Berkeley, CA. P. 585.

Heintzelman, Samuel P.
1852   Report, Reconnicance of the Gulf of California and
                Colorado River, 1850-51. 32nd Congress, 1st Session,
                Senate Executive Document 81. Washington.

Hill, Joseph J.
1923   Ewing Young in the Fur Trade of the Far Southwest,
                1822-1834. The Quarterly of the Oregon Historical
                Society XXIV(March).

Hoffman, Bvt. Lt. Colonel William
1860a   Report to General N. S. Clarke, Commander of the
                Military Department of California, January 16, 1859.
                Report of the Secretary of War, 1859. U.S. 36th Con-
                gress, 1st Session. HR Executive Document, Vol.
                II:389-392. Washington, D.C.: George W. Bowman,
                Printer.

1860b   Report to General Clarke, sent to Major William W.
                Mackall, April 24, 1859. Report of the Secretary of

War, 1859. U.S. 36th Congress, 1st Session. HR Executive Document, Vol. II:409. Washington, D.C.: George W. Bowman, Printer.

1860c   Report to General Clarke, sent to Major William W. Mackall, May 18, 1859. Report of the Secretary of War, 1859. U.S. 36th Congress, 1st Session. HR Executive Document, Vol. II:411-413. Washington, D.C.: George W. Bowman, Printer.

Ives, Joseph C.
1861   Report Upon the Colorado River of the West. Corps of Topographical Engineers. U. S. 36th Congress, 1st Session. Washington.

Kroeber, A. L. and C. B. Kroeber
1973   A Mohave War Reminiscence, 1854-1880. University of California Publications in Anthropology, Volume 10. Berkeley and Los Angeles: University of California Press.

Marshall, Thomas M.
1916   St. Vrain's Expedition to the Gila in 1826. The South-western Historical Quarterly XIX(January).

Meriam, C. H.
1923   The Route of Jedediah Smith in 1826. California Historical Society II(October).

Möllhausen, Baldwin
1858   Diary of a Journey from the Mississippi to the Coasts of the Pacific with a United States Government Expedition, with an Introduction by Alexander Von Humboldt. Translated by Mrs. Percy Sinnett. Vol. II. London: Longman, Brown, Green, Longmans, & Roberts. Reprinted by Johnson Reprint Company, N. Y., 1969).

Morgan, Dale L.
1953   Jedediah Smith and the Opening of the West. Indianapolis: Bobbs-Merrill.

Morgan, Dale L., and Carl I. Wheat
1954   Jedediah Smith and His Maps of the American West.
            San Francisco: California Historical Society.

Ogden, Peter Skene
1933   Traits of American Indian Life and Character, by a Fur
            Trader. San Francisco: Grabhorn Press.

Pattie, James O.
1831   The Personal Narrative of James O. Pattie: The Un-
            abridged Edition. Introduction by William H. Goetz-
            mann. Philadelphia and New York: J. B. Lippincott
            Company.

Priestly, Herbert I., ed.
1913   The Colorado River Campaign, 1781-1782; Diary of
            Pedro Fages. Publications of the Academy of Pacific
            Coast Hisory 3(2):101. Berkeley: University of Califor-
            nia.

Quaife, Milo M., ed.
1930   The Personal Narrative of James O. Pattie of Kentucky,
            1831 (ed. Timothy Flint). Chicago: Lakeside Press.

1935   Kit Carson's Autobiography. Chicago: Lakeside Press.

Rose, L.J.
1859   Letter to the editor, November 9. The Missouri Republi-
            can newspaper. Peosaquab, Iowa. Reprinted in Cleland,
            1951.

Rose, L. J., Jr.
1959   L. J. Rose of Sunny Slope. Pasadena: Castle Press.

Sherer, Lorraine M.
1965   The Clan System of the Fort Mojave Indians: A Con-
            temporary Survey. Southern California Quarterly. The
            Publication of the Historical Society of Southern Califor-
            nia, Volume XLVII, Number 1 (March), pp. 1-72.

1966   Great Chieftains of the Mojave Indians. Southern
            California Quarterly. The Publication of the Historical

Society of Southern California, Volume XLVIII, Number 1 (March), pp. 1-35.

1967a   The Name Mojave, Mohave: A History of Its Origin and Meaning. Southern California Quarterly. The Publication of the Historical Society of Southern California, Volume XLIX, Number 1, pp. 1-72.

1967b   The Name Mojave, Mohave: An Addendum. Southern California Quarterly. The Publication of the Historical Society of Southern California, Volume XLIX, Number 4 (December), pp. 455-458.

Sitgreaves, Captain Lorenzo
1854   Report of an Expedition Down the Zuni and Colorado Rivers. U.S. 33rd Cong., 1st Sess., U.S. Senate Executive Document. Washington: Beverley Tucker, Senate Printer.

Smith, Jedediah S.
n.d.   Journal, 1827. Manuscript in files of Smith family. Published in Sullivan 1934.

Stacey, May Humphreys
1929   Uncle Sam's Camels. The Journal of May Humphreys Stacey; Supplemented by the Report of Edward Fitzgerald Beale (1859), edited by Lewis B. Lesley.

Stillman, Frances
1988   Personal Communication to Vane and Bean.

1989   Personal Communication to Vane and Bean.

1990   Personal Communication to Vane and Bean.

1993   Personal Communication to Vane and Bean.

Sullivan, Maurice S., ed.
1934   The Travels of Jedediah Smith. Santa Ana: Fine Arts Press.

Thwaites, Reuben Gold, ed.
1905   Early Western Travels, 1748-1846, Vol. 18. Pattie's
              Personal Narrative, 1824-1830. Cleveland: Arthur C.
              Clark Co.

Udell, John
1859   Journal of John Udell. Yale University Library Reprint.
              Suisun City: Solano County Herald. Western Historical
              Series No. 1, December 1952.

U. S. Department of War
1858   Report of the Secretary of War. U. S. 35th Congress, 1st
              Session, Senate Executive Document No. 11. Washing-
              ton, D.C.: William A. Harris, Printer. Volume II.

1860   Report of the Secretary of War, 1859. U.S. 36th Con-
              gress, 1st Session. HR Executive Document. Washing-
              ton, D.C.: George W. Bowman, Printer. Volume II.

Whipple, Lt. Amiel Weeks
1856   Report Upon the Indian Tribes. In Reports of Explora-
              tions and Surveys to Ascertain the Most Practicable and
              Economical Route for a Railroad From the Mississippi
              River to the Pacific Ocean, 1853-4, Vol. 3. U.S. 33rd
              Cong., 2nd Sess., Executive Doc. No. 91. Washington:
              A.O.P. Nicholson.

White, Lieutenant J. L. and Party
1858   Report to Major W. W. Mackall, Assistant Adjutant
              General, U. S. Army, Department of California, of
              Exploration of Rio Colorado, January 30. Ms. in Hayes
              Collection, Bancroft Library, University of California,
              Berkeley.

Winder, Lt. Wm. A.
1857   Report to Major W. W. Mackall, Assistant Adjutant
              General, U. S. Army, Department of California, Decem-
              ber 31. Ms. in Hayes Collection, Bancroft Library,
              University of California, Berkeley.

Woodward, Arthur
1955   Feud on the Colorado. Los Angeles: Westernlore Press.

INDEX

Editorial: Orders: Ballena Press Publishers Services
Ballena Press   P.O. Box 2510
823 Valparaiso Avenue   Novato, CA 94948
Menlo Park, CA 94025   Tel. (415) 883-3530
Tel. (415) 323-9261   Fax: (415) 883-4280
Fax: (415) 321-2529

OTHER BALLENA TITLES